Open Economy Dynamics

Contributions to Economics

Michael Carlberg

Open Economy Dynamics

With 61 Figures

Physica-Verlag

A Springer-Verlag Company

Series Editors

Werner A. Müller

Peter Schuster

Author

Professor Dr. Michael Carlberg

Department of Economics

Federal University

Holstenhofweg 85

D-22043 Hamburg, Germany

A printing grant by Federal University, Hamburg, is gratefully acknowledged.

ISBN 3-7908-0708-7 Physica-Verlag Heidelberg

ISBN 0-387-91456-0 Springer-Verlag New York

CIP-Titelaufnahme der Deutschen Bibliothek
Carlberg, Michael:
Open economy dynamics / Michael Carlberg. – Heidelberg :
Physica-Verl., 1993
(Contributions to economics)
ISBN 3-7908-0708-7

PREFACE

The focus is on the interaction between demand and supply in a small open economy featuring the dynamics of private capital, public debt and foreign assets. The overlapping generations model serves as a microfoundation. It proves useful to consider different scenarios. Exchange rates are either flexible or fixed. Money wages can be flexible, fixed or slow. Monetary and fiscal policy may be exogenous or endogenous. Either budget deficits are allowed, or continuous budget balance is postulated. What are the implications of various shocks? How does the chain of cause and effect look like?

I had many helpful talks with my colleagues at Hamburg: Michael Schmid (now at Bamberg), Wolf Schäfer and Johannes Hackmann. In addition, Daphni—Marina Papadopoulou and Christine Schäfer—Lochte carefully discussed with me all parts of the manuscript. Last but not least, Doris Ehrich typed the manuscript as excellently as ever. I would like to thank all of them.

CONTENTS

"We are reluctant to recommend more research on deficits, given the already huge volume of literature on the subject. However, there seems to be room for analysis of the effects of persistent budget deficits in a greater variety of circumstances. For example, what are the consequences of unsustainable policies not reversed before the situation gets "out of hand"? Both the profession and the lay public need a plausible "doomsday scenario" in debating the needs for and merits of fiscal austerity programs."

Michael Haliassos
James Tobin

"If you want a high—investment, rapid—growth society, reverse the drift of fiscal and monetary policy. Over the business cycle as a whole, aim for budget surpluses. Turn more of the economy's cyclical management over to the Fed. Make sure that Congress resists the temptation to boost spending or cut taxes in recessions, and make sure that the Fed reacts as quickly to unemployment as it does to inflation."

Paul A. Samuelson
William D. Nordhaus

INTRODUCTION

The analysis will be conducted within an IS–LM model of a small open economy featuring the dynamics of money wages, private capital, public debt and foreign assets. A macroeconomic shock induces an extended process of adjustment that is characterized by unemployment. This in turn requires a dynamic path of monetary and fiscal policy: As a response to the shock, the central bank continuously adapts the quantity of money so as to keep up full employment all the time. And the government continuously accommodates its purchases of goods and services. Can this be sustained? Or will public and foreign debt tend to explode, thereby driving the stock of capital down to zero?

The study gives rise to a good deal of cases. Exchange rates are either flexible or fixed. Money wages can be flexible, fixed or slow. Policy may be fixed (exogenous), flexible or slow (endogenous). Either budget deficits are allowed, or continuous budget balance is postulated. In addition, a series of macroeconomic shocks can hit the economy: The foreign interest rate declines, labour supply increases, the propensity to save rises, the quantity of money contracts, exports come down, foreign prices are cut back, investment deteriorates, money wages spring up, public consumption expands, or domestic currency becomes devaluated.

Four sources of dynamics will be considered. Private investment serves to close the gap between the desired and the actual stock of capital round by round. Further the government levies taxes and raises loans in order to finance public consumption and the interest payments on public debt. And the budget deficit leads to the build-up of public debt. Moreover domestic residents earn interest on foreign assets. The excess of exports plus interest inflow over imports makes up the current account surplus. The current account surplus in turn contributes to the accumulation of foreign assets. Finally money wages react slowly to supply and demand in the labour market. In mathematical terms, this amounts to a system of four differential equations. By means of phase diagrams, we shall trace out the time paths of the state variables. How do aggregate demand, employment and capital move over time? What does the chain of cause and effect look like?

The approach of the present monograph can also be phrased from another perspective. Which theory is correct, Keynesian or neoclassical? What is the true model, IS–LM or growth? Several answers can be given to these questions. First, one of the approaches is right, whereas the other is wrong. Second, it depends on the situation. The economy is either in the Keynesian or in the neoclassical regime. And third, it is a matter of time horizon. Keynesian theory gives the short—run effects, while neoclassical theory presents the long—run effects. But how do we get from the short—run to the long—run equilibrium? It will be argued here that dynamic analysis permits a fusion of Keynesian and neoclassical theory.

In the literature on IS—LM dynamics, the underlying economy is either closed or open, and policy may be exogenous or endogenous. The present monograph departs from the seminal work done by Blinder and Solow (1973). The authors contemplate a closed economy with exogenous policy, focusing on government budget dynamics. Some years later, Scarth (1979), Cohen and de Leeuw (1980) as well as Smith (1982) proceed to a closed economy with endogenous policy. Monetary and fiscal policy are continuously adjusted so as to maintain full employment all the time.

The next point refers to an open economy with exogenous policy. A Keynesian analysis of current account dynamics is offered by Branson (1976), Turnovsky (1976), Buiter (1978), Allen and Kenen (1980), Aoki (1981) as well as Gandolfo (1986). In Allen and Kenen (1980), e. g., the portfolio consists of domestic money, domestic bonds and foreign bonds. Beyond that they distinguish between nontraded goods, export goods and import goods. Emphasis is laid on the dynamics of foreign assets and public debt, yielding a condition for long—run stability. By way of contrast, a neoclassical avenue is taken by Frenkel and Rodriguez (1975), Obstfeld (1981), Turnovsky (1981), Helpman and Razin (1982), Sachs (1982), Persson and Svensson (1985), Frenkel and Razin (1987), Siebert (1988) as well as Schmid (1990).

The open economy with endogenous policy, on the other hand, seems to be a rather neglected field of research, exceptions being Turnovsky (1979) and Klausinger (1986). Turnovsky starts from a small open economy with perfect capital mobility. The country suffers from underemployment, and prices are given. Current account dynamics and government budget dynamics propel the economy. There is no capital. At the center stage performs the slow policy mix. Under fixed exchange rates, fiscal policy should be directed at an income target, whereas monetary policy should be directed at a reserve target. Under flexible exchange rates, conversely, fiscal policy should aim at the exchange rate, while monetary policy should aim at income. Turnovsky, too, derives a condition for long—run stability.

The present monograph is composed of two major parts, flexible exchange rates (part I) and fixed exchange rates (part II). Each part in turn comprises two chapters, the basic model (chapter I) and the economy with public sector (chapter II).

Let us begin with the basic model under flexible exchange rates in chapter I of part I. It addresses the dynamics of foreign assets, private capital and money wages. First have a look at sections 1 until 3. As a base of comparison, we shall briefly sketch out the overlapping generations model. Then we shall establish an IS–LM model of a small open economy with perfect capital mobility. Here it proves useful to distinguish between the short–run equilibrium and the long–run equilibrium. We shall discuss the stability of the long–run equilibrium and keep track of the path generated by a macroeconomic shock. In doing this, money wages are supposed to be either flexible or fixed or slow. What is more, in section 4, we shall introduce monetary policy as a dynamic instrument to overcome a macroeconomic disturbance. In section 5, the analysis will be extended to include two countries. In section 6, we shall take account of capital gains on foreign assets, caused for instance by a depreciation. To conclude, in section 7, a portfolio model will be laid out in greater detail.

At this stage, we shall close chapter I and open up chapter II. There the public sector will enter the scene, adding the dynamics of public debt. As a frame of reference, in section 1, we shall install the overlapping generations model. Further, in sections 2 until 4, we shall set up an IS–LM model, exploring the dynamic effects of macroeconomic disruptions. Once more, money wages are flexible, fixed or slow. As an exception, in section 5, continuous budget balance will be assumed. In sections 6 until 8, we shall see whether monetary and fiscal policy are suited to absorb a macroeconomic shock. In section 9, two countries will be posited. At last, in section 10, we shall investigate a portfolio model. At this juncture, we shall move on from flexible to fixed exchange rates. The exposition of part II will be very similar to that of part I.

For the remainder of the introduction, we shall look into the exposition more closely. Let us begin with the basic model under flexible exchange rates in part I of chapter I. This is an IS–LM model augmented by the dynamics of foreign assets, private capital and money wages. In the short–run equilibrium, foreign assets, private capital and money wages are given exogenously. In the long–run equilibrium, on the other hand, these variables have adjusted completely.

First of all we shall inaugurate the short–run equilibrium. Firms produce a homogeneous commodity with the help of capital and labour. Domestic output equals the sum of consumption, investment and exports, diminished by imports. The investigation will be carried out within a small open economy characterized by perfect capital mobility. Therefore the domestic interest rate coincides with the foreign interest rate that is assumed to be constant. Firms maximize profits under perfect competition, so the marginal product of capital is determined by the interest rate. From this follows immediately the desired stock of capital. Analogously, the real wage rate corresponds to the marginal product of labour.

We come now to the laws of motion. Let us start with current account dynamics. Exports are an increasing function of the real exchange rate, while imports vary in proportion to consumption. Besides domestic residents earn interest on foreign assets. The current account surplus is defined as exports plus interest inflow minus imports. The current account surplus in turn adds to the stock of foreign assets. Next a few words will be said on investment dynamics. Investment serves to overcome the discrepancy between desired and actual capital period by period. The third point refers to savings dynamics. By virtue of overlapping generations, desired wealth is proportional to domestic income. And actual wealth comprises foreign assets as well as private capital. Then savings are used to bridge the gap between desired and actual wealth successively. Over and above that, domestic income and the interest inflow form the income of domestic residents, which can be devoted to consumption and savings. Last but not least, as far as wage dynamics are concerned, the rate of change of money wages is a decreasing function of the rate of unemployment. The real demand for money is positively correlated with income and negatively correlated with the interest rate. The central bank fixes the nominal quantity of money. In equilibrium, the real supply of money agrees with the real demand for it.

In summary, firms employ as many workers as they need to satisfy aggregate demand, given the stock of capital. Firms set prices such that real wages equal the marginal product of labour, given money wages. Prices in turn feed back on aggregate demand via the Keynes effect, hence the system is interdependent.

At this point, we leave the short—run equilibrium and enter the long—run equilibrium. What are the main properties of the long—run equilibrium? The current account balances, so foreign assets are no longer piled up. Firms abstain from investment, thus the stock of capital is uniform. And households refrain from saving, hence wealth does not accumulate any more. Owing to full employment, money wages stay put. And the level of output is invariant, since labour supply is exogenous. As a result, this is the steady state of a stationary economy. Now what are the long—run consequences of a monetary expansion? Foreign assets, private capital and output remain unaffected, yet money wages, prices and the exchange rate go up in proportion. That is to say, the monetary expansion has no real effects in the long run.

Here a comment is in place. Both in the short—run and in the long—run equilibrium, liquidity preference accords with the interest rate. In the short period, the marginal product of capital deviates from the interest rate, while in the long period they harmonize. The real wage rate, on the other hand, conforms with the marginal product of labour in the short term as well as in the long term. The short—run equilibrium is dominated by aggregate demand, whereas the long—run equilibrium is dominated by aggregate supply.

The short—run equilibrium can be represented by a system of three differential equations in foreign assets, private capital and money wages. By adopting phase diagram techniques, we shall probe into the stability of the long—run equilibrium. There it will be argued that a macroeconomic disturbance occasions a drawn—out process of adjustment. Take for example a monetary impulse. Initially the economy is in the steady state. Moreover let the foreign position be balanced. Against this background, the quantity of money contracts, say because there is a drop in the money multiplier. In the short run, domestic currency appreciates, thereby reducing exports and output. That is why unemployment emerges. The cut in exports brings the current account into deficit, and the fall in income lowers investment. In the medium run, owing to the current account deficit, foreign debt builds up round by round. And due to the negative investment, the stock of capital becomes dismantled step by step. On account of the unemployment, money wages start to decline. Competition forces firms to curtail prices, thus expanding real balances. The ensuing depreciation increases exports and output, so unemployment abates. In addition, the rise in income is accompanied by a rise in investment. This poses quite a lot of questions: After some time, will the deficit on current account turn into a surplus? Will investment become positive? Will the economy switch from underemployment to overemployment? Will the country gravitate to a new steady state? Along which paths will foreign debt and private capital evolve? So far money wages were supposed to be slow. What would happen if, instead, money wages were flexible or fixed?

In the preceding sections, we started from the premise that macroeconomic disruptions bring about unemployment. Now, in section 4, we shall deal with monetary policy, which offers a radical change of perspective. As a response to a shock, the central bank continuously adapts the quantity of money so as to defend full employment. Here the response may be either instantaneous or delayed. Is this feasible in the long run?

At this juncture, we come to chapter II where the public sector will be incorporated into the basic model. The government collects taxes and raises loans in order to cover its purchases of goods and services as well as the interest payments on public debt. Public borrowing in turn leads to the accumulation of public debt. Consider e.g. a monetary shock under fixed money wages. Originally the economy rests in the long—run equilibrium. The budget and the current account are balanced. Over and above that, let the labour market clear, and let there be neither public debt nor foreign assets. Under these circumstances, the quantity of money diminishes. In the short run, domestic currency appreciates. This deteriorates exports and output, giving rise to unemployment. By virtue of the decrease in exports, the current account moves into deficit. And the depression in income goes along with a depression in tax revenue, so the budget gets into deficit. In the medium run, owing to the budget deficit, public debt begins to pile up. Similarly, the current account deficit adds to foreign debt. What is more, the expansion of public debt entails an expansion of public interest, thereby enlarging the budget deficit. For that reason, the growth of public debt speeds up. And the accumulation of foreign debt broadens the interest outflow, thus aggravating the current account deficit. Therefore, foreign debt is built up more rapidly. In the long run, will public and foreign debt tend to explode? Will this boost the foreign interest rate up to infinity, squeezing domestic capital down to zero?

As a rule, public consumption and the tax rate are assumed to be given exogenously. As an exception, in section 5, we shall posit continuous budget balance. As a response to a shock, the government continuously accommodates public consumption so as to always balance the budget. What are the dynamic implications of this strategy? Then, in section 6, we shall return to monetary policy. As a response to a shock, the central bank continuously adjusts the quantity of money so as to maintain full employment at all times. In this situation, will public debt fatally crowd out private capital? Ultimately, in section 8, we shall combine monetary policy with continuous budget balance. To absorb a shock, the central bank continuously adapts the quantity of money so as to secure full employment all the time. And the government continuously accommodates public consumption so as to always balance the budget. Can this approach be sustained?

At this stage, we close flexible exchange rates in part I and open up fixed exchange rates in part II. First of all catch a glimpse of the basic model in chapter I. Regard for instance an export shock under fixed money wages. At the start, the economy is in the stationary state, in particular the current account balances. Beyond that, let all workers have a job, and let domestic residents hold no foreign assets. Against this background, exports decline spontaneously. In the short run, firms put a brake on output and dismiss workers. In the medium run, the current account deficit contributes to the accumulation of foreign debt. Accordingly, wealth, consumption and output come down, which reinforces unemployment. As far as the current account is concerned, there are two opposing tendencies. On the one hand, the fall in wealth, consumption and hence in imports lowers the current account deficit. On the other hand, the rise in foreign debt and the subsequent rise in interest outflow raise the current account deficit. What is the net effect? Eventually, will foreign debt proliferate without bounds? Will unemployment persist?

At last, in chapter II, the basic model will be extended to include the public sector. Contemplate for example an export shock under fixed money wages. Initially the economy is at rest in the long—run equilibrium. Besides let the labour market clear, and let there be neither public nor foreign debt. Under these circumstances, exports worsen autonomously. In the short run, firms reduce output and lay off workers. In the medium run, on account of the budget deficit, public debt starts to build up. And because of the current account deficit, foreign debt comes into existence. In the long run, will public and foreign debt grow without limits?

As an exception, in section 4, we shall require continuous budget balance. How will the process of adjustment be modified by this? Then, in section 5, we shall study fiscal policy. As a reaction to a shock, the government continuously adapts public consumption so as to always keep up full employment. On that grounds, will public debt displace private capital? Finally, in section 6, we shall join fiscal policy and continuous budget balance. To overcome a disturbance, the government continuously accommodates public consumption and the tax rate so as to maintain both full employment and budget balance at all times. Is this feasible in the long run?

PART I. FLEXIBLE EXCHANGE RATES

Chapter I. Basic Model

Let us begin with the basic model under flexible exchange rates. In the current chapter, the limelight will be on the dynamics of foreign assets, private capital and money wages. First of all have a look at sections 1 until 3. As a base of comparison, the overlapping generations model will be sketched out briefly. Then we shall establish the IS–LM model of a small open economy with perfect capital mobility. There it proves useful to distinguish between the short–run equilibrium and the long–run equilibrium. Further the stability of the long–run equilibrium will be verified. In addition we shall trace out the processes of adjustment induced by diverse macroeconomic shocks. In doing this, money wages are assumed to be either flexible, fixed or slow. In section 4, we shall inquire into monetary policy as a dynamic instrument to overcome a macroeconomic disturbance. In section 5, a second country will be incorporated into the analysis. In section 6, we shall allow for capital gains on foreign assets, caused e.g. by a depreciation. To conclude, in section 7, a portfolio model will be elaborated to some extent.

1. FLEXIBLE MONEY WAGES

1.1. OVERLAPPING GENERATIONS

In the current section, we shall present an overlapping generations model without bequests, confer Diamond 1965. It offers the monetary analysis of a stationary economy. The aim is to furnish a microfoundation for the (long–run equilibrium in the) basic model. Why do we postulate a stationary economy? For ease of exposition, without losing generality. And why overlapping generations? Because in a Solow model of a stationary economy, no steady state does exist.

Labour supply is assumed to be given exogenously $\overline{N}$ = const. In the long term, money wages are flexible so as to adapt labour demand N to labour supply $\overline{N}$:

$$N = \overline{N} \tag{1}$$

Put another way, full employment prevails forever. Firms manufacture a single commodity Y by means of capital K and labour N. More precisely, N denotes the number of active workers. To simplify matters, regard a Cobb–Douglas technology exhibiting constant returns to scale:

$$Y = K^{\alpha} N^{\beta} \tag{2}$$

with $\alpha > 0$, $\beta > 0$ and $\alpha + \beta = 1$. Domestic output Y can be dedicated to consumption C, investment I and exports X minus imports Q:

$$Y = C + I + X - Q \tag{3}$$

The investigation will be carried out within a small open economy, so the foreign interest rate is invariant $r^* $ = const. Moreover we grant perfect capital mobility, hence the domestic interest rate corresponds to the foreign interest rate $r = r^*$. Therefore the domestic interest rate is invariant, too. Firms maximize profits under perfect competition:

$$\Pi = pY - prK - wN \tag{4}$$

Here Π denotes profits, p the price of domestic goods and w the money wage rate. Differentiate (4) for K, set the derivative equal to zero and reshuffle:

$$r = \partial Y/\partial K = \alpha Y/K \tag{5}$$

That means, the marginal product of capital is determined by the interest rate. Similarly, the real wage rate coincides with the marginal product of labour:

$$w/p = \partial Y/\partial N = \beta Y/N \tag{6}$$

Exports are an increasing function of the real exchange rate:

$$X = (ep^*/p)^\theta \tag{7}$$

where e symbolizes the nominal exchange rate, p the price of domestic goods, p^* the price of foreign goods, ep^*/p the real exchange rate and θ the elasticity. For the small open economy, the price of foreign goods is external $p^* = $ const. Imports are proportionate to consumption:

$$Q = qC \tag{8}$$

with import rate $q = $ const. The trade surplus is defined as the excess of exports over imports:

$$H = X - Q \tag{9}$$

Domestic residents earn the interest rate r on foreign assets F, thus the interest inflow amounts to rF. Exports plus interest inflow minus imports constitute the current account surplus:

$$E = X + rF - Q \tag{10}$$

Foreign assets and the current account surplus this period give foreign assets next period:

$$F_{+1} = F + E \tag{11}$$

In the long–run equilibrium, foreign assets do no longer accumulate $F_{+1} = F$. In other words, the current account balances:

$$E = 0 \qquad (12)$$

As a corollary, we have $H + rF = 0$.

The individual lifecycle consists of two periods, of the working period and of the retirement period. During the working period, the individual receives labour income which he partly consumes and partly saves. The savings in turn are used to buy bonds. During the retirement period, the individual earns interest on the bonds and sells the bonds altogether. The proceeds are entirely consumed, no bequests are left.

The utility u of the representative individual depends on consumption per head in the working period c^1 and on consumption per head in the retirement period c^2. Take a logarithmic utility function:

$$u = \gamma \log c^1 + \delta \log c^2 \qquad (13)$$

with $\gamma > 0$, $\delta > 0$ and $\gamma + \delta = 1$. The budget constraint of the representative individual covers the whole lifecycle. w/p is labour income in the working period and $w/p - c^1$ are savings in the working period. The individual realizes the interest rate r on savings, so consumption in the retirement period is $(w/p - c^1)(1 + r) = c^2$. As a consequence, the individual budget constraint can be stated as:

$$c^1 + \frac{c^2}{1 + r} = \frac{w}{p} \qquad (14)$$

The individual chooses present and future consumption so as to maximize utility subject to its budget constraint. The evaluation of the Lagrange function yields consumption per head in the working period:

$$c^1 = \gamma w/p \qquad (15)$$

Labour income minus consumption per head provides savings per head $a = w/p - c^1$ or

$$a = \delta w/p \tag{16}$$

The savings of the active generation amount to $A = aN$. Observe (16) and (6) to arrive at:

$$A = \beta\delta Y \tag{17}$$

The savings of the young generation serve to finance foreign assets and domestic capital of the subsequent period:

$$F_{+1} + K_{+1} = A \tag{18}$$

In the long–run equilibrium, foreign assets and domestic capital do not grow any more $F_{+1} = F$ and $K_{+1} = K$. Insert this together with (17) into (18) to reach:

$$F + K = \beta\delta Y \tag{19}$$

Besides investment augments the stock of capital:

$$K_{+1} = K + I \tag{20}$$

In the steady state, the stock of capital is uniform, hence firms do not invest:

$$I = 0 \tag{21}$$

The next point refers to the money market. The real demand for money is an increasing function of income and a declining function of the interest rate $L = Y/r^{\eta}$ with interest elasticity η. The monetary authority controls the nominal quantity of money $M = $ const. The real supply of money matches the real demand for it, thus the money market clears:

$$M/p = Y/r^{\eta} \tag{22}$$

Incidentally, most of the variables are expressed in real terms, strictly speaking in units of domestic goods: A, C, F, I, K, Q, S, X and Y. Only e, p, w, and M are nominal variables.

In summary, the long–run equilibrium can be compressed into a system of ten equations:

$$Y = K^{\alpha} \overline{N}^{\beta} \tag{23}$$

$$r = \alpha Y/K \tag{24}$$

$$F + K = \beta \delta Y \tag{25}$$

$$H + rF = 0 \tag{26}$$

$$M/p = Y/r^{\eta} \tag{27}$$

$$w/p = \beta Y/\overline{N} \tag{28}$$

$$Y = C + H \tag{29}$$

$$H = X - Q \tag{30}$$

$$X = (ep^*/p)^{\theta} \tag{31}$$

$$Q = qC \tag{32}$$

α, β, δ, η, θ, p^*, q, r, M and $\overline{N}$ are fixed, whereas e, p, w, C, F, H, K, Q, X and Y adjust themselves appropriately. There are as many equations as unknowns, hence the solution is definite.

What are the salient features of the long–run equilibrium? All workers have got a job. The current account balances, so foreign assets stop to pile up. Firms refrain from investment, thus the stock of capital is uniform. Likewise households abstain from saving, hence wealth is constant. And output does not change, since labour supply is invariant. That is to say, this is the steady state of a stationary economy.

Having laid this groundwork, we shall solve the system (23) until (32) for the endogenous variables. First eliminate K in (23) with the help of (24) and rearrange:

$$Y = (\alpha/r)^{\alpha/\beta} \overline{N} \tag{33}$$

Then substitute this into $K = \alpha Y/r$ to obtain:

$$K = (\alpha/r)^{1/\beta} \overline{N} \tag{34}$$

Accordingly, a rise in the foreign interest rate lowers domestic capital and output. And an expansion in labour supply leads to a proportionate expansion in domestic capital and output.

Next insert $K = \alpha Y/r$ into (25) to get $F = (\beta\delta - \alpha/r)Y$. Further take account of (33) to arrive at:

$$F = (\beta\delta - \alpha/r)(\alpha/r)^{\alpha/\beta} \overline{N} \tag{35}$$

If $\delta \gtrless \alpha/\beta r$, then $F \gtrless 0$. Put differently, under a strong propensity to save, domestic residents will hold foreign assets. The other way round, under a weak propensity to save, domestic residents will owe money to foreigners. The inequality can be reformulated from another point of view. If $r \gtrless \alpha/\beta\delta$, then $F \gtrless 0$. That is, if the foreign interest rate is high, the country will be a creditor. Conversely, if the foreign interest rate is low, the country will be a debtor. Beyond that, if $r \gtrless \alpha/\beta\delta$, then $\partial F/\partial \overline{N} \gtrless 0$. Under a large interest rate, an increase in labour supply raises foreign assets. Under a small interest rate, however, an increase in labour supply raises foreign debt. Analogously, if $r \lessgtr \alpha/\beta\delta$, then $\partial F/\partial r \gtrless 0$. If the foreign interest rate is low, a boost in the foreign interest rate elevates foreign assets. On the other hand, if the foreign interest rate is sufficiently high, a boost in the foreign interest rate depresses foreign assets. As r approaches zero, F tends to minus infinity. And as r tends to plus infinity, F converges to zero. As a result, figure 1 shows foreign assets as a function of the foreign interest rate. How does this relate to a closed economy? For $F = 0$, (25) can be written as $K = \beta\delta Y$. This together with (24) yields $r = \alpha/\beta\delta$. As long as the foreign interest rate stays close to $\alpha/\beta\delta$, a boost in the foreign interest rate enhances foreign assets.

Now get rid of F in (26) by making use of (35):

$$H = (\alpha - \beta\delta r)(\alpha/r)^{\alpha/\beta} \overline{N} \tag{36}$$

If $r \lessgtr \alpha/\beta\delta$, then $H \gtrless 0$. Under a low interest rate, the country will experience a trade surplus. Yet under a high interest rate, the country will incur a trade deficit. Further combine (33) and (36) with $Y = C + H$, from which follows:

$$C = (\beta + \beta\delta r)(\alpha/r)^{\alpha/\beta} \overline{N} \tag{37}$$

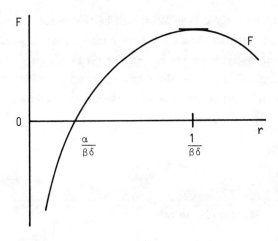

Figure 1
Foreign Interest Rate and
Foreign Assets

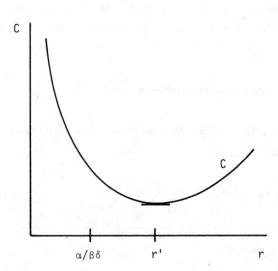

Figure 2
Foreign Interest Rate and Consumption

If $r \lessgtr \alpha/(\delta - 2\alpha\delta)$, then $\partial C/\partial r \lessgtr 0$. What will be the impact on consumption of a rise in the foreign interest rate? When the foreign interest rate is small, consumption will come down. Conversely, when the foreign interest rate is large, consumption will go up. Correspondingly figure 2 visualizes how consumption varies with the foreign interest rate. In the relevant range, near $\alpha/\beta\delta$, the curve is downward sloping. Moreover put (33) into (27) and regroup:

$$p = \frac{r^{\eta}M}{(\alpha/r)^{\alpha/\beta}\,\overline{N}} \tag{38}$$

Similarly substitute (33) into (28) to gain:

$$w/p = \beta(\alpha/r)^{\alpha/\beta} \tag{39}$$

In addition eliminate p in (39) by means of (38):

$$w = \frac{\beta r^{\eta}M}{\overline{N}} \tag{40}$$

Over and above that, we shall deduce exports. First take account of (30) and (32) in (29) to conclude $Y = (1 - q)C + X$. Then allow für $C = (\beta + \beta\delta r)Y$, which yields $X = [1 - (1-q)(\beta + \beta\delta r)]Y$. Finally pay attention to (33):

$$X = [1 - (1 - q)(\beta + \beta\delta r)](\alpha/r)^{\alpha/\beta}\,\overline{N} \tag{41}$$

From the empirical point of view, the term in square brackets seems to be positive. Next insert (37) into (32):

$$Q = (\beta + \beta\delta r)(\alpha/r)^{\alpha/\beta}q\overline{N} \tag{42}$$

Besides compare the real exchange rate $R = ep^*/p$ with (31) to ascertain $X = R^{\theta}$ and note (41):

$$R^{\theta} = [1 - (1 - q)(\beta + \beta\delta r)](\alpha/r)^{\alpha/\beta}\,\overline{N} \tag{43}$$

Last but not least, we shall try to find out the nominal exchange rate. To begin

with, substitute (31) and (32) into (30), for ease of exposition letting $\theta = 1$, to attain
$H = ep^*/p - qC$. After that put this into (29): $Y = (1 - q)C + ep^*/p$. Eventually
observe $C = (\beta + \beta\delta r)Y$ as well as (27) $p = r^\eta M/Y$ and solve for the nominal exchange rate:

$$e = [1 - (1 - q)(\beta + \beta\delta r)]r^\eta M/p^* \tag{44}$$

Building on this foundation, what are the long–run implications of macroeconomic shocks? First consider a monetary expansion. This disturbance leaves no impact
on capital, output, foreign assets, consumption, exports, imports and the balance of
trade. Only money wages, prices and the nominal exchange rate move up in proportion. In other words, domestic currency depreciates in nominal terms. Real wages
and the real exchange rate remain unaffected. As a result, the monetary expansion
has no real effects in the long–run. Second have a look at an increase in the foreign
interest rate. Capital, output, exports and the trade surplus decline. Locally foreign
assets rise, while consumption and imports fall. Money wages and prices are marked
up, but real wages and the real exchange rate are cut down. That means, the shock
leads to a real appreciation.

Third regard an addition to labour supply. This raises capital, output and consumption in proportion. Locally, foreign assets and the trade balance do not respond.
Both exports and imports are elevated. Money wages and prices are depressed proportionately, yet the nominal exchange rate is uniform, at least locally. Real wages
stay put, whereas the real exchange rate shifts upwards. There will be a real depreciation. Fourth contemplate a rise in the "propensity to save" δ. This disruption has
no influence on capital and output. It increases foreign assets, consumption and
imports, but reduces exports and the trade surplus. Money wages as well as prices
hold fast, and the nominal exchange rate comes down. Real wages remain untouched, and the real exchange rate is lowered. Table 1 offers a synopsis of the
long–run consequences.

Table 1
Long–Run Effects (Flexible Money Wages)

	M ↑	r* ↑	$\overline{N}$ ↑	δ ↑
K	→	↓	↑	→
Y	→	↓	↑	→
F	→	↑	→	↑
C	→	↓	↑	↑
X	→	↓	↑	↓
Q	→	↓	↑	↑
H	→	↓	→	↓
w	↑	↑	↓	→
p	↑	↑	↓	→
e	↑	?	→	↓
w/p	→	↓	→	→
ep*/p	→	↓	↑	↓

1.2. SHORT–RUN EQUILIBRIUM AND LONG–RUN EQUILIBRIUM

The process of adjustment can be viewed as a sequence of temporary equilibria that converge to a permanent equilibrium. In the short–run equilibrium, foreign assets and domestic capital are given exogenously. In the long–run equilibrium, however, they have adjusted completely.

Let us begin with the short–run equilibrium. Labour supply is assumed to be invariant $\overline{N}$ = const. Money wages are flexible, so labour demand agrees with labour supply $N = \overline{N}$. That is to say, there will always be full employment. Firms produce a homogeneous commodity Y by means of capital K and labour N. For the sake of simplicity, consider a Cobb–Douglas technology $Y = K^{\alpha}N^{\beta}$ with $\alpha > 0$, $\beta > 0$ and $\alpha + \beta = 1$. Firms produce as much as households, firms and foreigners want to buy $Y = C + I + X - Q$. Here Y denotes domestic output, C consumption, I investment, X exports and Q imports. The analysis will be implemented within a small open economy characterized by perfect capital mobility, hence the domestic interest rate r coincides with the foreign interest rate r* that is fixed $r = r^* = $ const. Firms maximize profits $\Pi = pY - prK - wN$ under perfect competition. As a consequence, the marginal product of capital is determined by the interest rate $r = \partial Y/\partial K = \alpha Y/K$. From this one can immediately derive the desired stock of capital $K^* = \alpha Y/r$. Likewise the real wage rate corresponds to the marginal product of labour $w/p = \partial Y/\partial N = \beta Y/N$.

Now have a look at investment dynamics. Investment serves to close the gap between desired capital K* and actual capital K round by round $I = \lambda(K^* - K)$, where $0 < \lambda < 1$ stands for the speed of adjustment. In this way investment adds to the stock of capital $\dot{K} = I$. Here the dot symbolizes the time derivative $\dot{K} = dK/d\tau$ with time τ. The next point refers to current account dynamics. Exports are an increasing function of the real exchange rate $X = (ep^*/p)^{\theta}$. Here e denotes the nominal exchange rate, p the price of domestic goods, p* the price of foreign goods, ep*/p the real exchange rate and θ the elasticity. For the small open economy, the price of foreign goods belongs to the data $p^* = $ const. Imports are proportionate to consumption $Q = qC$ with import rate $q = $ const. The trade surplus can be defined as the difference between exports and imports $H = X - Q$. Domestic residents earn the interest rate r on foreign assets F, so the interest inflow totals rF. Exports plus interest inflow minus imports give the current account surplus $E = X + rF - Q$. The current account surplus in turn contributes to the accumulation of foreign assets $\dot{F} = E$. Finally a few remarks will be made on savings dynamics. According to overlapping generations, desired wealth is proportionate to domestic income $A^* = \beta\delta Y$, cf. section 1.1. And actual wealth comprises foreign assets as well as domestic capital $A = F + K$. Then savings are used to overcome the discrepancy between desired and actual wealth period by period $S = \mu(A^* - A)$, where $0 < \mu < 1$ stands for the velocity of adaptation. Savings in turn lead to the formation of wealth $\dot{A} = S$. Domestic income and the interest inflow make up the income of domestic residents, which can be devoted to consumption and savings $Y + rF = C + S$.

With respect to the money market we start from the following premise. The real demand for money is positively correlated with income and negatively correlated with the interest rate $L = Y/r^\eta$. The central bank fixes the nominal quantity of money $M = $ const. In equilibrium, the real supply of money equals the real demand for it $M/p = Y/r^\eta$. Note that money does not enter the wealth identity. The reason is that money is created by an open market operation. In other words, the central bank acquires bonds that represent capital. Including both the stock of capital and the stock of money would amount to double counting.

In summary the short–run equilibrium can be described by a system of fifteen equations:

$$Y = C + I + X - Q \tag{1}$$

$$Y = K^\alpha N^\beta \tag{2}$$

$$K^* = \alpha Y/r \tag{3}$$

$$I = \lambda(K^* - K) \tag{4}$$

$$\dot{K} = I \tag{5}$$

$$X = (ep^*/p)^\theta \tag{6}$$

$$Q = qC \tag{7}$$

$$\dot{F} = X + rF - Q \tag{8}$$

$$Y + rF = C + S \tag{9}$$

$$S = \mu(A^* - A) \tag{10}$$

$$A^* = \beta\delta Y \tag{11}$$

$$A = F + K \tag{12}$$

$$N = \overline{N} \tag{13}$$

$$w/p = \beta Y/N \tag{14}$$

$$M/p = Y/r^\eta \tag{15}$$

Here α, β, δ, η, θ, λ, μ, p^*, q, r, F, K, M and $\overline{N}$ are given exogenously, while e, p, w, $\dot{A}$, A^*, C, $\dot{F}$, I, K^*, K, N Q, S, X and Y are accommodated suitably.

Further substitute (11) and (12) into (10) to obtain the savings function:

$$S = \beta\delta\mu Y - \mu(F + K) \tag{16}$$

Moreover eliminate S in (9) with the help of (16) to get the consumption function:

$$C = (1 - \beta\delta\mu)Y + rF + \mu(F + K) \tag{17}$$

On that grounds, an increase in domestic income raises both savings and consumption. The building up of wealth discourages savings and stimulates consumption. Conversely, a rise in the propensity to save elevates savings and depresses consumption. Besides insert (2) together with (13) into (15) and solve for the price of domestic goods:

$$p = \frac{r^\eta M}{K^\alpha \overline{N}^\beta} \tag{18}$$

Put differently, a monetary expansion inflates prices. On the other hand, capital formation reduces prices.

At this stage we leave the short–run equilibrium and come to the long–run equilibrium. Obviously, the short–run quilibrium can be condensed to a system of two differential equations:

$$\dot{F} = f(F, K) \tag{19}$$

$$\dot{K} = g(F, K) \tag{20}$$

In the long–run equilibrium, foreign assets and domestic capital cease to move:

$$\dot{F} = \dot{K} = 0 \tag{21}$$

Owing to (21) and (5), firms do no longer invest $I = 0$. That is why (4) can be written as $K^* = K$. Combine this with (3) to achieve

$$r = \alpha Y/K \tag{22}$$

which reminds one of overlapping generations. Beyond that compare (1) and (9), paying heed to $I = 0$, to reach $S = X + rF - Q$. In conjunction with (8) this yields $\dot{F} = S$. Due to $\dot{F} = 0$ it holds $S = 0$. Now put this into (10) to gain $A^* = A$. At last, taking account of (11) and (12), one arrives at:

$$F + K = \beta \delta Y \tag{23}$$

Again this confirms the conclusions drawn for overlapping generations. As a result, the long–run equilibrium is identical to that obtained under overlapping generations. For the main properties of the steady state see section 1.1.

1.3. STABILITY

By adopting phase diagram techniques, we shall discuss the stability of the long–run equilibrium. Let us begin with the $\dot{K} = 0$ demarcation line. Equate $\dot{K} = I$ and $I = \lambda\,(K^* - K)$, observing $K^* = \alpha Y/r$ and $Y = K^\alpha\,\overline{N}^\beta$:

$$\dot{K} = \lambda(\alpha K^\alpha\,\overline{N}^\beta/r - K) \tag{1}$$

Now differentiate (1) for K and evaluate the derivative at the long–run equilibrium with $K = (\alpha/r)^{1/\beta}\,\overline{N}$ to gain $d\dot{K}/dK = -\beta\lambda < 0$. Then set (1) equal to zero and solve for

$$K = (\alpha/r)^{1/\beta}\,\overline{N} \tag{2}$$

Therefore the $\dot{K} = 0$ line is horizontal, see figures 1 and 2.

Next we shall ascertain the $\dot{F} = 0$ demarcation line. The comparison of $Y = C + I + X - Q$ and $Y + rF = C + S$ provides $S - I = X + rF - Q$. By virtue of $\dot{F} = X + rF - Q$, one can deduce $\dot{F} = S - I$. Further we shall try to find out the savings function and the investment function. Get rid of A^* and A in $S = \mu(A^* - A)$ by taking account of $A^* = \beta\delta Y$, $Y = K^\alpha\,\overline{N}^\beta$ and $A = F + K$ to conclude:

$$S = \beta\delta\mu K^\alpha\,\overline{N}^\beta - \mu(F + K) \tag{3}$$

Similarly combine $I = \lambda(K^* - K)$, $K^* = \alpha Y/r$ and $Y = K^\alpha\,\overline{N}^\beta$:

$$I = \lambda(\alpha K^\alpha\,\overline{N}^\beta/r - K) \tag{4}$$

Moreover substitute (3) and (4) into $\dot{F} = S - I$ to accomplish:

$$\dot{F} = \beta\delta\mu K^\alpha\,N^\beta - \mu(F + K) - \lambda(\alpha K^\alpha\,N^\beta/r - K) \tag{5}$$

Accordingly it is valid that $\partial\dot{F}/\partial F = -\mu < 0$. In addition set (5) equal to zero and state explicitly:

$$\mu F = \beta\delta\mu K^{\alpha}\overline{N}^{\beta} - \mu K - \alpha\lambda K^{\alpha}\overline{N}^{\beta}/r + \lambda K \tag{6}$$

Then differentiate (6) for K and appraise the derivative at the steady state to arrive at the critical interest rate $r' = (\mu - \beta\lambda)/\beta\delta\mu$. As a standard, consider the closed economy with $r = \alpha/\beta\delta$. If $\lambda \lesseqgtr \mu$, then $dF/dK \lesseqgtr 0$. Henceforth we shall assume that as a rule capital is adjusted less rapidly than wealth $\lambda < \mu$. This implies $dF/dK < 0$, so the $\dot{F} = 0$ line is downward sloping, confer figure 1.

Taking all pieces together, figure 1 contains the phase diagram. As a principal result, the long–run equilibrium proves to be stable. Finally what will be the impact of various shocks in the phase diagram? Due to (2) and (6), a monetary expansion has no influence on F and K, thus both demarcation lines stay put. An increase in the interest rate lowers K and raises F, thereby shifting the $\dot{K} = 0$ line downwards and the $\dot{F} = 0$ line to the right. An addition to labour supply enhances both K and F. As a consequence, the $\dot{K} = 0$ line travels upwards, while the $\dot{F} = 0$ line glides to the right. A rise in the propensity to save does not affect K yet lifts F. The $\dot{K} = 0$ line remains fixed, and the $\dot{F} = 0$ line moves to the right. As an exception, figure 2 portrays the case $\lambda > \mu$. In this instance, too, the steady state turns out to be stable.

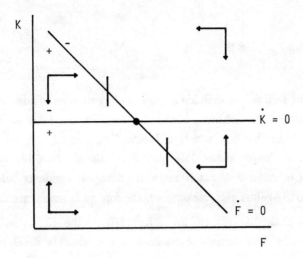

Figure 1
Dynamics of Foreign Assets and
Domestic Capital ($\lambda < \mu$)

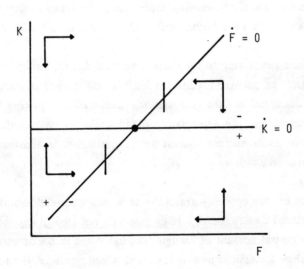

Figure 2
Dynamics of Foreign Assets and
Domestic Capital ($\lambda > \mu$)

1.4. SHOCKS

In the current section, we shall keep track of the processes of adjustment generated by diverse macroeconomic disturbances. First consider an interest shock. Initially the economy is in the long–run equilibrium. The current account balances, so foreign assets do no longer accumulate. And firms abstain from investment, hence domestic capital is uniform. What is more, let domestic residents hold no foreign assets at the start. Against this background, the foreign interest rate declines spontaneously. In the phase diagram, the $\dot{F} = 0$ line shifts to the left, whereas the $\dot{K} = 0$ line travels upwards. The streamline graphs how the economy develops over time, see figure 1.

In the short run, as a consequence, capital flows in. Domestic currency appreciates, thereby impeding exports. On the other hand, the domestic interest rate is cut back, thus fostering investment. The net effect is to reduce aggregate demand, output and employment. In other words, unemployment emerges. Because of this, money wages drop instantaneously. Competition forces firms to lower prices, which raises real balances. Due to the ensuing depreciation, exports and aggregate demand recover. In the short–run equilibrium, on balance, output is still at its original level.

In the medium run, owing to the current account deficit, foreign debt builds up step by step. And the positive investment leads to the growth of domestic capital. The expansion of capital in turn decreases marginal cost and prices. Therefore the rise of real balances and the depreciation of domestic currency continue. Exports recover even more, so the current account deficit diminishes. In addition, investment subsides as capital accumulates.

As time goes on, the economy gravitates to a new long–run equilibrium. Again the current account balances, hence foreign assets do not change any more. Properly speaking, a substantial amount of foreign debt has come into existence. And firms stop to invest, thus domestic capital is invariant. More precisely, the terminal stock of capital clearly exceeds the initial stock.

Second we shall address a labour supply shock. At the beginning, the economy rests in the steady state. Under these circumstances, labour supply increases autono-

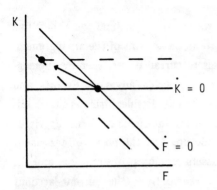

Figure 1
Interest Shock

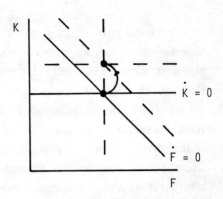

Figure 2
Labour Supply Shock

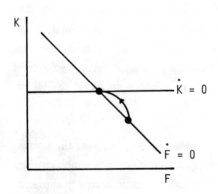

Figure 3
Investment Shock

mously. In the phase diagram, the $\dot{F} = 0$ line goes to the right, and the $\dot{K} = 0$ line moves upwards, compare figure 2. In the short term, on account of the arising unemployment, money wages fall. This compels firms to curtail prices, thereby augmenting real balances. Domestic currency depreciates, which advances exports and output. The expansion of income stimulates investment. Besides firms engage additional workers, thus restoring full employment. In the intermediate term, by virtue of the current account surplus, foreign assets pile up. And the positive investment starts capital formation. The accumulation of assets promotes consumption, and the subsequent appreciation impairs exports. After some time, the current account surplus turns into a deficit, so foreign assets begin again to decline. Further the growth of capital dampens investment. In due course, the economy converges to a new steady state. Ultimately domestic residents hold no foreign assets, while the stock of capital is larger than before.

Third have a look at a savings shock. Originally the economy is in the stationary state. In this situation, the preference for future consumption δ climbs. In the phase diagram, the $\dot{F} = 0$ line glides to the right. In the short run, this disruption pushes up savings and pulls down both consumption and aggregate demand. The ensuing depreciation improves exports and aggregate demand, thus income stays put. In the medium run, owing to the current account surplus, foreign assets build up. The addition to wealth is an incentive for consumption. This is accompanied by an appreciation that deteriorates exports, hence the current account surplus dwindles away. Eventually the economy reaches a new stationary state. A certain volume of foreign assets has been heaped up during transition, whereas domestic capital remains fixed.

Fourth take a monetary disturbance. Initially the economy rests in the permanent equilibrium. Against this background, the quantity of money contracts, say because the money multiplier drops. In the short period, domestic currency appreciates, which worsens exports, aggregate demand, output and employment. That means, unemployment occurs. As a response, money wages are cut back immediately. The deflation of prices enhances real balances, and the resulting depreciation encourages exports. In the temporary equilibrium, both exports and output are at the baseline. Merely the exchange rate, prices and money wages went down in proportion. To conclude, the monetary disruption has no real effects, neither in the short run nor in the long run. In the phase diagram, nothing happens.

Fifth catch a glimpse of an export shock. At the start, the economy is in the steady state. Under these circumstances, exports come down exogenously. In the phase diagram, nothing occurs. In the short term, domestic currency depreciates, thereby restoring exports endogenously. For that reason, the disturbance leaves no impact, neither in the short term nor in the long term. Sixth regard a foreign price shock. At the beginning, once more, the economy is in the stationary state. In this situation, the price of foreign goods declines. In the phase diagram, nothing takes place. In the short period, the disruption lowers exports. As an instantaneous answer, domestic currency depreciates, which raises exports to the original level. On that grounds, the impulse has no real consequences, neither in the short period nor in the long period.

Last but not least we shall deal with an investment shock. Initially the economy is in the long—run equilibrium. Then, suddenly, investment deteriorates. In the short run, domestic currency depreciates, so exports improve, while output remains unaffected. The negative investment reduces domestic capital, and the current account surplus increases foreign assets. In the medium run, investment recovers endogenously, and the subsequent appreciation brings exports down again. Due to the positive investment, domestic capital is replenished round by round. And owing to the current account deficit, foreign assets are returned piecemeal. Ultimately the economy comes back to its starting point. The streamline plots how the economy travels through time, cf. figure 3.

2. FIXED MONEY WAGES

2.1. OVERLAPPING GENERATIONS

In the current section we postulate fixed money wages. Apart from this we take the same approach as before. As a point of departure, consider the long–run equilibrium under flexible money wages, cf. equations (23) until (32) in section 1.1. The only difference is that here $Y = K^{\alpha}N^{\beta}$ is substituted for (23), and that $w/p = \beta Y/N$ takes the place of (28).

Hence the long–run equilibrium can be represented by a system of ten equations:

$$Y = K^{\alpha}N^{\beta} \tag{1}$$

$$r = \alpha Y/K \tag{2}$$

$$F + K = \beta\delta Y \tag{3}$$

$$H + rF = 0 \tag{4}$$

$$M/p = Y/r^{\eta} \tag{5}$$

$$w/p = \beta Y/N \tag{6}$$

$$Y = C + H \tag{7}$$

$$H = X - Q \tag{8}$$

$$X = (ep^*/p)^{\theta} \tag{9}$$

$$Q = qC \tag{10}$$

Here α, β, δ, η, θ, p^*, q, r, w and M are given, whereas e, p, C, F, H, K, N, Q, X and Y adjust themselves appropriately. Money wages are exogenous while labour demand is endogenous, as opposed to the case of flexible money wages. As an implication, the economy will generally suffer from unemployment (or overemployment).

Now what are the salient features of the long–run equilibrium under fixed money wages? As mentioned above, unemployment will prevail. The current account balances, so foreign assets do no longer pile up. Firms abstain from investment, thus domestic capital is constant. And output is uniform since labour demand does not change any more. Again this is the steady state of a stationary economy.

At this juncture we shall solve the system (1) until (10) for the endogenous variables. First combine (5) and (6) to reach:

$$N = \frac{r^{\eta}\beta M}{w} \tag{11}$$

Then insert (2) $K = \alpha Y/r$ into (1), paying attention to (11):

$$Y = \frac{\alpha^{\alpha/\beta}\beta M}{r^{\alpha/\beta-\eta}w} \tag{12}$$

Next eliminate Y in $K = \alpha Y/r$ by means of (12):

$$K = \frac{\alpha^{1/\beta}\beta M}{r^{1/\beta-\eta}w} \tag{13}$$

Further (3) in conjunction with (2) yields $F = (\beta\delta - \alpha/r)Y$. Get rid of Y with the help of (12) to obtain:

$$F = \frac{\alpha^{\alpha/\beta}(\beta\delta - \alpha/r)\beta M}{r^{\alpha/\beta-\eta}w} \tag{14}$$

If $r \gtrless \alpha/\beta\delta$, then $F \gtrless 0$. That is to say, if the foreign interest rate is high, domestic residents hold foreign assets. The other way round, if the foreign interest rate is low, domestic residents owe money to foreigners. Moreover, how is the foreign position affected by a monetary expansion? If $r \gtrless \alpha/\beta\delta$, then $\partial F/\partial M \gtrless 0$. In other words, under a large interest rate, foreign assets rise. Conversely, under a small interest rate, it is foreign debt that rises. Another point refers to an increase in the foreign interest rate itself. If $r \lessgtr \alpha(1 - \beta\eta)/\beta\delta(\alpha - \beta\eta)$, then $\partial F/\partial r \gtrless 0$. As long as the foreign interest rate stays below the critical level, this enhances foreign assets. However, as soon as the foreign interest rate surpasses the critical level, this depresses foreign assets. Compare this to a closed economy where it is valid that $r = \alpha/\beta\delta$. Provided the foreign interest rate comes close to $\alpha/\beta\delta$, the boost in the foreign interest rate elevates foreign assets.

In addition put $Y = (\alpha/r)^{\alpha/\beta} N$ into (6):

$$w/p = \beta(\alpha/r)^{\alpha/\beta} \tag{15}$$

Besides state p explicitly:

$$p = (r/\alpha)^{\alpha/\beta} w/\beta \tag{16}$$

Beyond that solve (4) for H and take account of (14):

$$H = \frac{\alpha^{\alpha/\beta}(\alpha - \beta\delta r)\beta M}{r^{\alpha/\beta - \eta}w} \tag{17}$$

Now consumption will be derived. To begin with, join (4) and (7) $C = Y + rF$. Then observe $F = (\beta\delta - \alpha/r)Y$ and rearrange $C = (\beta + \beta\delta r)Y$. Finally note (12):

$$C = \frac{\alpha^{\alpha/\beta}(\beta + \beta\delta r)\beta M}{r^{\alpha/\beta - \eta}w} \tag{18}$$

Over and above that we shall verify exports. $Y = C + X - Q$ together with $Q = qC$ furnishes $X = Y - (1 - q)C$. Substitute (12) and (18) to gain:

$$X = \frac{[1 - (1 - q)(\beta + \beta\delta r)]\alpha^{\alpha/\beta}\beta M}{r^{\alpha/\beta - \eta}w} \tag{19}$$

(9) can be written as $R^\theta = X$, where R denotes the real exchange rate. Accordingly, (19) determines the real exchange rate. Coming to an end, the nominal exchange rate will be ascertained. For $\theta = p^* = 1$, (9) simplifies to $e = pX$. At last pay heed to (16) and (19):

$$e = [1 - (1 - q)(\beta + \beta\delta r)]r^\eta M \tag{20}$$

To conclude, we shall present an overview of the results obtained so far, confer table 2. What are the long–run consequences of macroeconomic shocks? First consider a monetary expansion. As a response, the following variables go up in proportion: domestic capital, labour demand, output, consumption, exports, imports, the nominal exchange rate and the real exchange rate. That means, domestic currency depreciates both in nominal terms and in real terms. On the other hand, foreign assets and the trade balance remain unchanged, at least locally. Prices and real wages are not altered. As a result, indeed, the monetary expansion has real effects. This is in clear opposition to the case of flexible money wages, where the disturbance had merely nominal effects. Second suppose that the foreign interest rate rises spontaneously. This lowers domestic capital, given $1/\beta > \eta$, which empirically seems to be sound. Similarly this lowers output, granted $\alpha/\beta > \eta$, which seems to be fulfilled, too. By way of contrast, this raises labour demand unequivocally. Foreign assets accumulate, whereas the trade surplus declines, both locally. Likewise exports, real wages and the real exchange rate come down, while prices are marked up.

Third we are concerned with an increase in the preference for future consumption δ. The disruption has no influence on domestic capital, labour demand and output. Foreign assets, consumption and imports mount, but exports and the trade surplus descend. Prices and real wages stay put, yet the exchange rate drops, in nominal terms as well as in real terms. Fourth contemplate an autonomous lift of money wages. The shock reduces the following variables in inverse proportion: domestic capital, labour demand, output, consumption, exports and imports. The other way round, the shock inflates prices in proportion. Locally, foreign assets and the trade balance hold fast. The nominal exchange rate and real wages do not react, while the real exchange rate declines.

Table 2
Long—Run Effects (Fixed Money Wages)

	$M \uparrow$	$r^* \uparrow$	$\delta \uparrow$	$w \uparrow$
K	↑	↓	→	↓
N	↑	↑	→	↓
Y	↑	↓	→	↓
F	→	↑	↑	→
C	↑	?	↑	↓
X	↑	↓	↓	↓
Q	↑	?	↑	↓
H	→	↓	↓	→
p	→	↑	→	↑
e	↑	?	↓	→
w/p	→	↓	→	→
ep^*/p	↑	↓	↓	↓

2.2. SHORT–RUN EQUILIBRIUM AND LONG–RUN EQUILIBRIUM

As a baseline, regard the short–run equilibrium under flexible money wages, confer equations (1) until (15) in section 1.2. The only difference is that in the current section money wages are exogenous whereas labour demand becomes endogenous. That is why (13) does not apply. Generally the economy will be characterized by underemployment (or overemployment).

Therefore the short–run equilibrium can be encapsulated in a system of fourteen equations:

$$Y = C + I + X - Q \tag{1}$$

$$Y = K^{\alpha}N^{\beta} \tag{2}$$

$$K^* = \alpha Y/r \tag{3}$$

$$I = \lambda(K^* - K) \tag{4}$$

$$\dot{K} = I \tag{5}$$

$$X = (ep^*/p)^{\theta} \tag{6}$$

$$Q = qC \tag{7}$$

$$\dot{F} = X + rF - Q \tag{8}$$

$$Y + rF = C + S \tag{9}$$

$$S = \mu(A^* - A) \tag{10}$$

$$A^* = \beta\delta Y \tag{11}$$

$$A = F + K \tag{12}$$

$$w/p = \beta Y/N \tag{13}$$

$$M/p = Y/r^{\eta} \tag{14}$$

Here α, β, δ, η, θ, λ, μ, p^*, q, r, w, F, K and M are given, while e, p, A, A^*, C, $\dot{F}$, I, K^*, $\dot{K}$, N, Q, S, X and Y accommodate themselves. The consumption function reminds one of that derived for flexible money wages $C = (1 - \beta\delta\mu)Y + \mu(F + K) +$

rF. Hence an increase in foreign assets or domestic capital raises consumption.

In summary, firms employ as many workers as they need to satisfy aggregate demand, given the stock of capital. Firms set prices such that real wages equal the marginal product of labour, given money wages. Prices in turn feed back on aggregate demand via the Keynes effect, hence the system is interdependent.

The short—run equilibrium can be condensed to a system of two differential equations $\dot{F} = f(F, K)$ and $\dot{K} = g(F, K)$. In the long—run equilibrium, foreign assets and domestic capital do no longer vary $\dot{F} = \dot{K} = 0$. What is more, the long—run equilibrium is identical to that obtained for overlapping generations, cf. equations (1) until (10) in section 2.1. There the main properties of the long—run equilibrium have been stated in greater detail. The proof follows the same lines as under flexible money wages, see section 1.2.

2.3. STABILITY

By making use of phase diagrams, we shall probe into the stability of the long—run equilibrium. Let us begin with the $\dot{K} = 0$ demarcation line. At first combine $\dot{K} = I$, $I = \lambda(K^* - K)$ and $K^* = \alpha Y/r$ to accomplish $\dot{K} = \lambda(\alpha Y/r - K)$. Then solve $w/p = \beta Y/N$ for N and eliminate pY with the help of $M/p = Y/r^{\eta}$ to reach $N = r^{\eta}\beta M/w$. Moreover substitute this into the production function:

$$Y = K^{\alpha}(r^{\eta}\beta M/w)^{\beta} \tag{1}$$

On that grounds, $\dot{K} = \lambda(\alpha Y/r - K)$ can be reformulated as:

$$\dot{K} = \lambda[\alpha K^{\alpha}(r^{\eta}\beta M/w)^{\beta}/r - K] \tag{2}$$

Further differentiate (2) for K and evaluate the derivative at the long—run equilibrium with $K = \alpha^{1/\beta}\beta M/r^{1/\beta - \eta}w$. In this way, one verifies that $\partial\dot{K}/\partial K = -\beta\lambda < 0$. Finally set $\dot{K} = 0$ in (2) and reshuffle:

$$K = \frac{\alpha^{1/\beta}\beta M}{r^{1/\beta - \eta}w} \tag{3}$$

Thus the $\dot{K} = 0$ line is horizontal, confer figures 1 and 2.

Now we come to the $\dot{F} = 0$ demarcation line. The comparison of $Y = C + I + X - Q$ and $Y + rF = C + S$ yields $S - I = X + rF - Q$. Next amalgamate this with $\dot{F} = X + rF - Q$ to gain $\dot{F} = S - I$. To get rid of S and I, insert $A^* = \beta\delta Y$ and $A = F + K$ into $S = \mu(A^* - A)$:

$$S = \beta\delta\mu Y - \mu(F + K) \tag{4}$$

In addition, from $I = \lambda(K^* - K)$ and $K^* = \alpha Y/r$ one can deduce $I = \lambda(\alpha Y/r - K)$. Put this in conjunction with (4) into $\dot{F} = S - I$, taking account of (1):

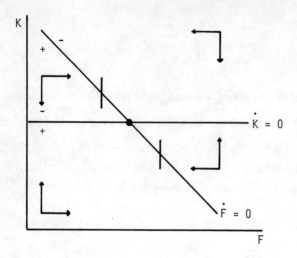

Figure 1
Dynamics of Foreign Assets and Domestic Capital ($\lambda < \mu$)

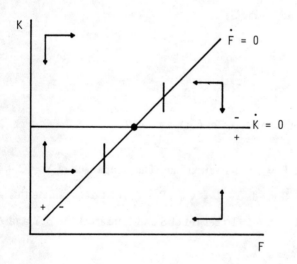

Figure 2
Dynamics of Foreign Assets and Domestic Capital ($\lambda > \mu$)

$$\dot{F} = (\beta\delta\mu - \alpha\lambda/r)K^{\alpha}(r^{\eta}\beta M/w)^{\beta} - \mu F + (\lambda - \mu)K \tag{5}$$

Besides differentiate (5) for F, which provides $\partial\dot{F}/\partial F = -\mu < 0$.

Beyond that set (5) equal to zero:

$$\mu F = (\beta\delta\mu - \alpha\lambda/r)K^{\alpha}(r^{\eta}\beta M/w)^{\beta} + (\lambda - \mu)K \tag{6}$$

Then differentiate (6) for K and try to find out the local value of the derivative. After some steps this leads to the critical level of the interest rate $r' = (\mu - \beta\lambda)/\beta\delta\mu$. As a point of reference consider the closed economy where it is valid that $r = \alpha/\beta\delta$. For that reason assume $r = \alpha/\beta\delta$. Correspondingly, if $\lambda \lesseqgtr \mu$, then $dF/dK \lesseqgtr 0$. Throughout we suppose that capital is slower to adapt than wealth $\lambda < \mu$, which involves $dF/dK < 0$. That is to say, the $\dot{F} = 0$ line is negatively inclined, see figure 1.

Assembling all component parts, figure 1 contains the phase diagram. As a basic result, the long–run equilibrium proves to be stable. As an exception, figure 2 shows the case $\lambda > \mu$. In this situation, too, the steady state turns out to be stable.

Last but not least, a few remarks will be made on how shocks are reflected by the phase diagram. First imagine a monetary expansion. Owing to (3) and (6), both K and F climb. That is why the $\dot{K} = 0$ line shifts upwards, yet the $\dot{F} = 0$ line shifts to the right. Second catch a glimpse of a boost in the foreign interest rate. This disturbance lowers K and raises F. As a consequence, the $\dot{K} = 0$ line moves downwards, while the $\dot{F} = 0$ line moves to the right. Third, an increase in the propensity to save leaves no impact on K, whereas it elevates F. Hence the $\dot{K} = 0$ line stays put, and the $\dot{F} = 0$ line travels to the right. Fourth, a lift in money wages depresses both K and F, thereby pulling the $\dot{K} = 0$ line downwards and pushing the $\dot{F} = 0$ line to the left.

2.4. SHOCKS

Here we shall keep track of the processes of adjustment generated by diverse macroeconomic shocks in greater detail. First consider a monetary disturbance. Initially the economy is in the long—run equilibrium. The current account balances, so foreign assets do neither accumulate nor decumulate. Firms abstain from investment, hence domestic capital is uniform. Over and above that, at the start, let the labour market clear, and let domestic residents hold no foreign assets. Against this background, the quantity of money contracts, say because the money multiplier drops. In the phase diagram, the $\dot{F} = 0$ line glides to the left, and the $\dot{K} = 0$ line glides downwards. The streamline in figure 1 visualizes how the economy moves over time.

In the short run, the disruption incites a capital inflow, thereby appreciating domestic currency. This lowers exports, aggregate demand, output and employment. That means, the economy will suffer from unemployment. Besides the reduction in exports brings the current account into deficit, and the diminution in income is associated with a diminution in investment.

In the medium run, the current account deficit builds up foreign debt round by round. And due to the negative investment, domestic capital becomes dismantled. In addition, the decline in capital drives up marginal cost. This forces firms to raise prices, thus contracting real balances even further. Therefore exports and output continue to fall. In the AD—AS diagram, this is tantamount to an upward shift of the AS curve. Both the accumulation of foreign debt and the decumulation of domestic capital reduce wealth. That is why consumption and imports diminish. After a certain span of time, the current account deficit turns into a surplus. As soon as this happens, foreign debt is being retired period by period. And to the extent that the stock of capital comes down, investment recovers.

Ultimately the economy attains a new long—run equilibrium. In the first place, unemployment will persist. Again the current account balances, so foreign assets stop changing. Strictly speaking, foreign debt will be paid back completely. Again firms refrain from investment, so domestic capital is invariant. More precisely, the terminal stock of capital stays below the initial one. To sum up, the monetary im-

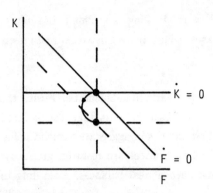

Figure 1
Monetary Shock

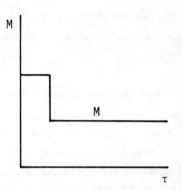

Figure 2
Quantity of Money

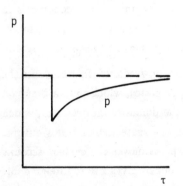

Figure 3
Prices

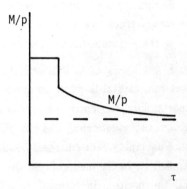

Figure 4
Real Balances

pulse has real effects, in the short run as well as in the long run. This is in remarkable contrast to the case of flexible money wages, where there existed no real effects at all.

Now have a look at the time paths of selected variables. Let us begin with the autonomous path of the quantity of money, see figure 2. Next take the induced movement of domestic prices in figure 3. At first the cut in aggregate demand deflates prices. Later on, owing to the decline of capital, prices are restored gradually. Then figure 4 displays the accompanying time path of real balances. According to figure 5, domestic currency appreciates both in the short term and in the intermediate term. Figure 6 illustrates the response of exports. The time path of the current account can be divided into two phases, cf. figures 7 and 8. During the first phase, the current account registers a deficit, thereby piling up foreign debt. During the second phase, the current account gets into surplus, thus amortizing foreign debt. Similarly figures 9 and 10 exhibit the stock adjustment of investment and capital. Figure 11 graphs the trajectory of output and income. Likewise figure 12 confronts the time paths of labour demand and supply. Moreover figures 13 and 14 present the stock adjustment of savings and wealth. At last figure 15 reveals the dynamics of consumption (and imports).

Second we are concerned with an interest shock. Originally the economy is in the steady state. All workers have got a job, and the foreign position is balanced. Under these circumstances, the foreign interest rate declines. In the phase diagram, the $\dot{F} = 0$ line goes to left, and the $\dot{K} = 0$ line goes upwards, cf. figure 16. In the short run, capital flows in, so domestic currency appreciates, which puts a brake on exports. Simultaneously the capital inflow reduces the domestic interest rate, which encourages investment. The net effect is to lower aggregate demand and output, hence unemployment emerges. Besides the fall in exports moves the current account into deficit. In the medium run, the current account deficit gives rise to foreign debt. And the positive investment adds to the stock of capital. Beyond that, capital growth brings down marginal cost and prices, thus augmenting real balances. The ensuing depreciation stimulates exports, which mitigates the current account deficit. As the stock of capital is adapted successfully, investment subsides. Asymptotically the economy tends to a new steady state. Still unemployment prevails. During transition, foreign debt has been accumulated, and domestic capital is greater than before.

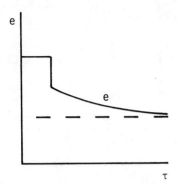

Figure 5
Exchange Rate

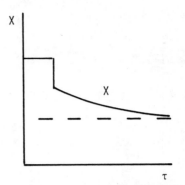

Figure 6
Exports

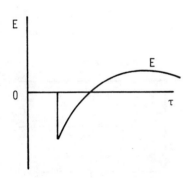

Figure 7
Current Account Surplus

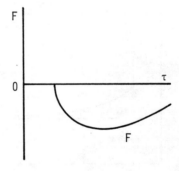

Figure 8
Foreign Assets

48

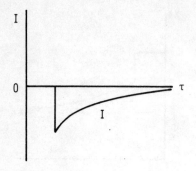

Figure 9
Investment

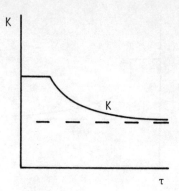

Figure 10
Capital

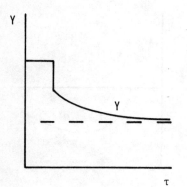

Figure 11
Income

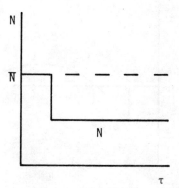

Figure 12
Labour Demand and
Labour Supply

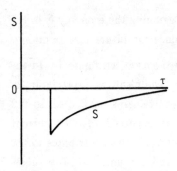

Figure 13
Savings

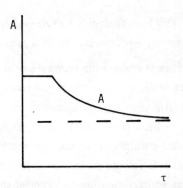

Figure 14
Wealth

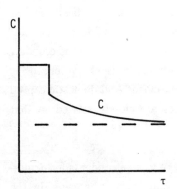

Figure 15
Consumption

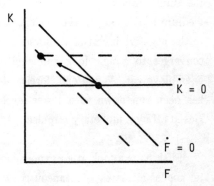

Figure 16
Interest Shock

Third we deal with a savings disruption. At the beginning the economy is in the stationary equilibrium. In this situation, the preference for future consumption δ rises. In the phase diagram, the $\dot{F} = 0$ line travels to the right, cf. figure 17. In the short term, savings mount yet consumption descends. The resulting depreciation of domestic currency advances exports. On balance output remains unaffected, so full employment continues to exist. Further the increase in exports leads to a current account surplus. In the medium term, the current account surplus contributes to the growth of foreign assets. This in turn raises wealth and consumption. The subsequent appreciation lowers exports, thereby reducing the current account surplus. In due course the economy approaches a new stationary equilibrium. The labour market still clears. A specific volume of foreign assets has been heaped up, while domestic capital was invariant.

Fourth we tackle a wage shock: Suddenly money wages are lifted. In the phase diagram, the $\dot{F} = 0$ line shifts to the left, whereas the $\dot{K} = 0$ line shifts downwards, which is reminiscent of the monetary disturbance in figure 1. In the short run, firms have to mark up prices, thus contracting real balances. The ensuing capital inflow appreciates domestic currency, which curtails exports and output. Therefore unemployment occurs. The decline in exports brings the current account into deficit, and the diminution in income is associated with a diminution in investment. In the medium run, owing to the current account deficit, foreign debt builds up. And due to the negative investment, domestic capital dwindles away. Over time the economy converges to a new long—run equilibrium that unfortunately is characterized by unemployment. At the end, foreign debt is entirely redeemed. And domestic capital has been run down to a lower level. These dynamics are closely related to that kicked off by a monetary impulse.

Fifth have a look at an export shock: The demand of foreign residents for domestic goods decreases spontaneously. In the phase diagram nothing happens. In the short period, domestic currency depreciates, which restores exports. Output does not react, hence all workers have still got a job. To conclude, the export disturbance has no real consequences, neither in the short period nor in the long period.

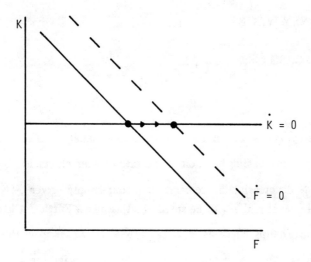

Figure 17
Savings Shock

3. SLOW MONEY WAGES

3.1. SPECIAL CASE I = 0

Now wage dynamics will be incorporated into the analysis. The rate of change of money wages is a decreasing function of the rate of unemployment $\dot{w}/w = - \epsilon(\overline{N} - N)/\overline{N}$, where N denotes labour demand, $\overline{N}$ labour supply (given), $(\overline{N} - N)/\overline{N}$ the rate of unemployment and $\epsilon > 0$ the speed of adjustment. Further it is convenient to reformulate the Phillips curve as $\dot{w} = \epsilon w(N/\overline{N} - 1)$. Apart from this we take the same approach as before. As compared to flexible money wages, $\dot{w} = \epsilon w(N/\overline{N} - 1)$ is substituted for $N = \overline{N}$. In addition, to simplify matters, let be $I = 0$, so K does not vary.

Accordingly the short—run equilibrium can be described by a system of twelve equations:

$$Y = C + X - Q \tag{1}$$

$$Y = K^{\alpha}N^{\beta} \tag{2}$$

$$X = (ep^*/p)^{\theta} \tag{3}$$

$$Q = qC \tag{4}$$

$$\dot{F} = X + rF - Q \tag{5}$$

$$Y + rF = C + S \tag{6}$$

$$S = \mu(A^* - A) \tag{7}$$

$$A^* = \beta\delta Y \tag{8}$$

$$A = F + K \tag{9}$$

$$\dot{w} = \epsilon w(N/\overline{N} - 1) \tag{10}$$

$$w/p = \beta Y/N \tag{11}$$

$$M/p = Y/r^{\eta} \tag{12}$$

Here α, β, δ, η, θ, μ, p^*, q, r, w, F, K, M and $\overline{N}$ are exogenous, whereas e, p, $\dot{w}$, A, A^*, C, $\dot{F}$, N, Q, S, X and Y are endogenous.

Moreover the short—run equilibrium can be compressed into a system of two differential equations:

$$\dot{w} = f(w, F) \tag{13}$$

$$\dot{F} = g(w, F) \tag{14}$$

In the long—run equilibrium, money wages and foreign assets cease to move:

$$\dot{w} = \dot{F} = 0 \tag{15}$$

Next a few words will be said on the steady state. Owing to (15), (10) can be written as $N = \overline{N}$. Together with (2) this yields $Y = K^\alpha \overline{N}^\beta$. Besides combine (11) and $N = \overline{N}$ to reach $w = \beta pY/\overline{N}$. Then eliminate pY by means of (12) to arrive at:

$$w = r^\eta \beta M/\overline{N} \tag{16}$$

This confirms the conclusions drawn for flexible money wages. Beyond that confront (1) and (6) to gain $X + rF - Q = S$. Now insert this into (5) to see $\dot{F} = S$. Again this is identical to the results obtained for flexible money wages. Due to (15) it applies $S = 0$. Put this into (7) to get $A = A^*$. Observing (8) and (9), one can deduce $F + K = \beta\delta Y$. Finally, in conjunction with $Y = K^\alpha \overline{N}^\beta$, this provides:

$$F = \beta\delta K^\alpha \overline{N}^\beta - K \tag{17}$$

What are the long—run consequences of a monetary expansion? Domestic output and foreign assets do not respond. Only money wages, prices and the exchange rate go up in proportion. That means, the disturbance has no real effects in the long run.

At this juncture, we shall inquire into the stability of the long—run equilibrium. First have a look at the $\dot{F} = 0$ demarcation line. To begin with, join $\dot{F} = S$ and $S =$

$\beta\delta\mu Y - \mu(F + K)$:

$$\dot{F} = \beta\delta\mu Y - \mu(F + K) \tag{18}$$

In the next step, get rid of Y. For that purpose, solve (11) for N, paying attention to pY from (12) $N = r^{\eta}\beta M/w$. Then substitute this into (2):

$$Y = K^{\alpha}(r^{\eta}\beta M/w)^{\beta} \tag{19}$$

Further amalgamate (19) with (18) to accomplish:

$$\dot{F} = \beta\delta\mu K^{\alpha}(r^{\eta}\beta M/w)^{\beta} - \mu(F + K) \tag{20}$$

Besides differentiate (20) for F to verify $\partial\dot{F}/\partial F = -\mu < 0$. In addition set (20) equal to zero and regroup $F = \beta\delta K^{\alpha}(r^{\eta}\beta M/w)^{\beta} - K$. By virtue of $dw/dF < 0$, the $\dot{F} = 0$ line is downward sloping, see figure 1. Second consider the $\dot{w} = 0$ demarcation line. Insert $N = r^{\eta}\beta M/w$ into (10):

$$\dot{w} = r^{\eta}\beta\epsilon M/\overline{N} - \epsilon w \tag{21}$$

Then take the derivative $\partial\dot{w}/\partial w = -\epsilon < 0$. Moreover set (21) equal to zero and reshuffle terms $w = r^{\eta}\beta M/\overline{N}$. For that reason, the $\dot{w} = 0$ line is horizontal. Putting all pieces together, we achieve the phase diagram in figure 1. As a corollary, the long–run equilibrium proves to be stable.

For the remainder of this section, we shall trace out the process of adjustment kicked off by a monetary shock. Initially the economy rests in the steady state. In particular, the labour market clears. The current account balances, so foreign assets do neither accumulate nor decumulate. What is more, let foreign assets be zero at the start. Against this background, the quantity of money diminishes spontaneously. In the phase diagram, the $\dot{F} = 0$ line shifts to the left, while the $\dot{K} = 0$ line shifts downwards, cf. figure 2. In the short term, domestic currency appreciates, which puts a brake on exports and output. That is why unemployment comes into existence. And the fall in exports brings the current account into deficit.

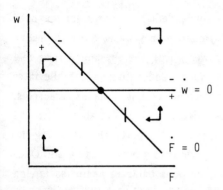

Figure 1
Dynamics of Foreign Assets
and Money Wages

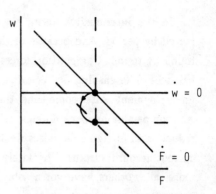

Figure 2
Monetary Shock

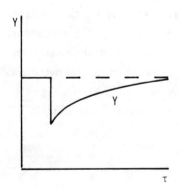

Figure 3
Output

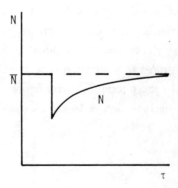

Figure 4
Labour Demand and
Labour Supply

In the intermediate term, the current account deficit increases foreign debt period by period. And because of the unemployment, money wages begin to decline round by round. Competition forces firms to lower prices, thereby augmenting real balances. The ensuing depreciation stimulates exports and output, which alleviates unemployment. After some time, the deficit on current account turns into a surplus. As soon as this happens, foreign debt becomes redeemed. Over and above that, the reduction in foreign debt raises wealth, consumption and imports, thus lessening the current account surplus. Ultimately the economy tends to a new steady state. Once more, all workers have got a job. The current account balances again, so foreign assets are constant. Strictly speaking, foreign debt will be paid back completely.

Last but not least, we shall throw some light on the accompanying time paths. At first the monetary impulse depresses output, cf. figure 3. Later on output recovers, asymptotically coming back to the baseline. In full analogy, figure 4 shows the trajectory of labour demand. The time path of the current account is composed of two phases, cf. figures 5 and 6. During the first phase, the current account gets into deficit, thus building up foreign debt. During the second phase, the current account changes into surplus, hence amortizing foreign debt. In the same vein, figures 7 and 8 portray the dynamics of savings and wealth. Figures 9 and 10 graph the slow adjustment of money wages and prices. And figure 11 reveals the associated movement of real wages. As far as the nominal exchange rate is concerned, the time path can be divided into two stages, cf. figure 12. At the beginning, the disturbance sharply cuts down the nominal exchange rate. Over time the nominal exchange rate is restored to a certain extent. In other words, the nominal exchange rate overshoots in the short term. Likewise figure 13 plots the trajectory of the real exchange rate. To conclude, figures 14 and 15 visualize the reaction of exports and consumption.

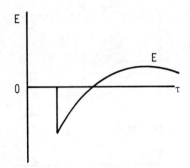

Figure 5
Current Account Surplus

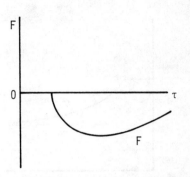

Figure 6
Foreign Assets

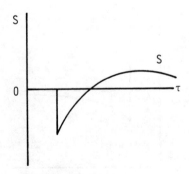

Figure 7
Savings

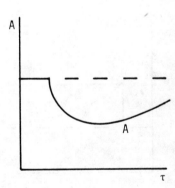

Figure 8
Wealth

58

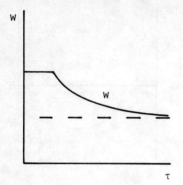

Figure 9
Money Wages

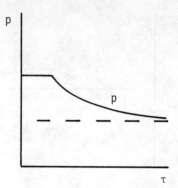

Figure 10
Prices

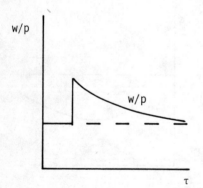

Figure 11
Real Wages

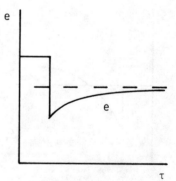

Figure 12
Nominal Exchange Rate

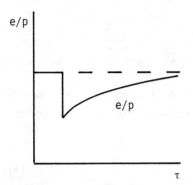

Figure 13
Real Exchange Rate

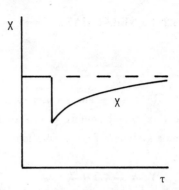

Figure 14
Exports

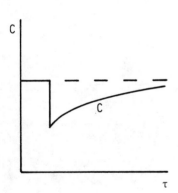

Figure 15
Consumption

3.2. GENERAL CASE

In the current section, we return to the standard assumption that domestic capital is endogenous. Correspondingly the short–run equilibrium can be represented by a system of fifteen equations:

$$Y = C + I + X - Q \tag{1}$$

$$Y = K^{\alpha} N^{\beta} \tag{2}$$

$$K^* = \alpha Y/r \tag{3}$$

$$I = \lambda(K^* - K) \tag{4}$$

$$\dot{K} = I \tag{5}$$

$$X = (ep^*/p)^{\theta} \tag{6}$$

$$Q = qC \tag{7}$$

$$\dot{F} = X + rF - Q \tag{8}$$

$$Y + rF = C + S \tag{9}$$

$$S = \mu(A^* - A) \tag{10}$$

$$A^* = \beta\delta Y \tag{11}$$

$$A = F + K \tag{12}$$

$$\dot{w} = \epsilon w(N/\overline{N} - 1) \tag{13}$$

$$w/p = \beta Y/N \tag{14}$$

$$M/p = Y/r^{\eta} \tag{15}$$

Here α, β, δ, η, θ, λ, μ, p^*, q, r, w, F, K, M and $\overline{N}$ are given, while e, p, $\dot{w}$, A, A^*, C, $\dot{F}$, I, K^*, $\dot{K}$, N, Q, S, X and Y adapt themselves.

The short–run equilibrium can be condensed to a system of three differential equations $\dot{w} = f(w, F, K)$, $\dot{F} = g(w, F, K)$ and $\dot{K} = h(w, F, K)$. In the long–run equilibrium it holds $\dot{w} = \dot{F} = \dot{K} = 0$. As an implication, the long–run equilibrium under slow money wages agrees with the long–run equilibrium under flexible money wages. What is more, the long–run equilibrium under slow money wages turns out to be stable. This underlines the importance of the conclusions drawn for flexible and fixed money wages.

Here a comment is in place. Liquidity preference accords with the interest rate, both in the short term and in the long term. In the short term, the marginal product of capital deviates from the interest rate. In the long term, on the other hand, they harmonize. And real wages conform with the marginal product of labour, both in the short term and in the long term. In summary, the short–term equilibrium is governed by aggregate demand, whereas the long–term equilibrium is dominated by aggregate supply.

Now we shall probe into the dynamics of a monetary disruption. Initially the economy is in the stationary equilibrium. Above all, full employment prevails. The current account balances, so foreign assets do not vary. And firms abstain form investment, so the stock of capital is uniform. Without losing generality, domestic residents hold no foreign assets. Under these circumstances, the quantity of money contracts. In the short run, domestic currency appreciates, which curtails exports and output. Therefore unemployment emerges. The diminution in exports moves the current account into deficit. And the drop in income is associated with a drop in investment.

In the medium run, due to the current account deficit, foreign debt grows step by step. And owing to the negative investment, the stock of capital withers away. Because of the unemployment, money wages and prices begin to decline, thereby expanding real balances. The subsequent depreciation boosts exports and output, hence unemployment recedes. And the rise in income goes along with a rise in investment. After some time, the deficit on current account is transformed into a surplus, thus foreign debt starts to decrease. And by virtue of the positive investment, the stock of capital recovers. In spite of that, the economy will not switch to overemployment. The underlying reason is that savings are high on account of the wealth gap, so consumption is low. Both the decumulation of foreign debt and the accumulation of domestic capital raise wealth, consumption and imports. This in turn reduces the current account surplus. Besides, as the stock of capital becomes restored, investment subsides.

Eventually the economy gravitates to a new stationary equilibrium. Full employment is regained. Once more the current account balances, hence foreign assets do not change. Similarly firms do no longer invest, thus the stock of capital is invariant. More exactly, the whole of foreign debt has been retired. And the stock of capital reaches its initial size.

The time paths are isomorphic to those derived for the special case $I = 0$. Of course the only exception is given by investment and the stock of capital. The process of adjustment can be split up into two stages, cf. figures 1 and 2. During the first stage investment is negative, so the stock of capital deteriorates. During the second stage investment becomes positive, thus replenishing the stock of capital.

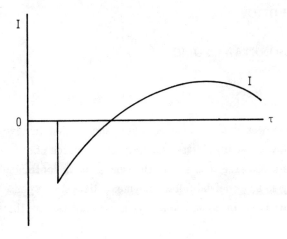

Figure 1
Investment

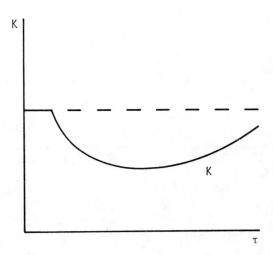

Figure 2
Capital

4. MONETARY POLICY

4.1. FLEXIBLE MONETARY POLICY

So far emphasis was laid on macroeconomic shocks that involve problems like unemployment. Now we shall address monetary policy which offers a radical change of perspective. As a response to a shock, the central bank continuously adjusts the quantity of money so as to defend full employment. Here the response may be either instantaneous or delayed. In doing the analysis, we shall assume that money wages answer slowly.

Let us begin with flexible monetary policy. At once the central bank adapts the quantity of money so as to maintain full employment at all times $N = \overline{N}$. As a corollary there is no reason why money wages should change. The short–run equilibrium can be set out as a system of fifteen equations:

$$Y = C + I + X - Q \tag{1}$$

$$Y = K^{\alpha}N^{\beta} \tag{2}$$

$$K^* = \alpha Y/r \tag{3}$$

$$I = \lambda(K^* - K) \tag{4}$$

$$\dot{K} = I \tag{5}$$

$$X = (ep^*/p)^{\theta} \tag{6}$$

$$Q = qC \tag{7}$$

$$\dot{F} = X + rF - Q \tag{8}$$

$$Y + rF = C + S \tag{9}$$

$$S = \mu(A^* - A) \tag{10}$$

$$A^* = \beta\delta Y \tag{11}$$

$$A = F + K \tag{12}$$

$$N = \overline{N} \tag{13}$$

$$w/p = \beta Y/N \tag{14}$$

$$M/p = Y/r^{\eta} \qquad\qquad (15)$$

Here α, β, δ, η, θ, λ, μ, p^*, q, r, w, F, K and $\overline{N}$ are exogenous, while e, p, A, A^*, C, $\dot{F}$, I, K^*, $\dot{K}$, M, N, Q, S, X and Y are endogenous.

The short–run equilibrium can be encapsulated in a system of two differential equations $\dot{F} = f(F, K)$ and $\dot{K} = g(F, K)$. Further the long–run equilibrium is subject to $\dot{F} = \dot{K} = 0$. In real terms, the long–run equilibrium coincides with that obtained for flexible money wages. As a result, the long–run equilibrium will be stable. This can be demonstrated in the same way as under flexible money wages.

To illustrate this, regard an interest shock. Initially the economy is at rest in the steady state. In particular, the labour market clears. Let domestic residents hold no foreign assets. In this situation, the foreign interest rate is cut back. In the short term, capital flows in, which appreciates domestic currency, so exports come down. On the other hand, the domestic interest rate declines, thereby pushing up investment. The net effect is to lower aggregate demand and output, giving rise to unemployment. Instantaneously, in order to prevent this, the central bank runs a loose monetary policy. The concomitant depreciation enhances exports, aggregate demand and output. The short–term equilibrium is characterized by full employment, the current account experiences a deficit, and investment is positive.

In the intermediate term, the current account deficit leads to the accumulation of foreign debt. And the positive investment starts capital formation. Besides the increase in capital entails an increase in full–employment output $\overline{Y} = K^{\alpha} \overline{N}^{\beta}$. Granted that the addition to aggregate demand falls short of the addition to full–employment output, monetary policy must be even more easy, and the other way round. In due course, the economy converges to a new steady state. Still all workers have got a job. The foreign position will again be balanced, and domestic capital will be higher than before. Figure 1 exhibits the required path of monetary policy. In summary, flexible monetary policy succeeds in always keeping up full employment. In a similar manner, monetary policy can absorb a monetary shock, a labour supply shock, a savings shock and a wage shock.

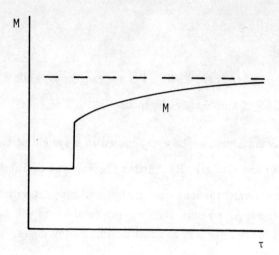

Figure 1
Flexible Monetary Policy

4.2. SLOW MONETARY POLICY

With a time lag, the central bank accommodates the quantity of money so as to restore full employment. More precisely, if the rate of unemployment goes up, then the rate of monetary expansion will go up as well, and vice versa $\dot{M}/M = \kappa[(\overline{N} - N)/\overline{N}]$, where $\kappa > 0$ symbolizes the speed of adjustment. The policy rule can be restated as $\dot{M} = \kappa M(1 - N/\overline{N})$. For the sake of convenience, we suppose that there is no investment and that money wages are fixed.

Therefore the short–run equilibrium can be described by a system of twelve equations:

$$Y = C + X - Q \tag{1}$$

$$Y = K^{\alpha}N^{\beta} \tag{2}$$

$$X = (ep^*/p)^{\theta} \tag{3}$$

$$Q = qC \tag{4}$$

$$\dot{F} = X + rF - Q \tag{5}$$

$$Y + rF = C + S \tag{6}$$

$$S = \mu(A^* - A) \tag{7}$$

$$A^* = \beta\delta Y \tag{8}$$

$$A = F + K \tag{9}$$

$$w/p = \beta Y/N \tag{10}$$

$$M/p = Y/r^{\eta} \tag{11}$$

$$\dot{M} = \kappa M(1 - N/\overline{N}) \tag{12}$$

Here α, β, δ, η, θ, κ, μ, p^*, q, r, w, F, K, M and $\overline{N}$ are given, whereas e, p, A, A^*, C, $\dot{F}$, $\dot{M}$, N, Q, S, X and Y adapt themselves.

The short–run equilibrium can be interpreted as a system of two differential equations:

$$\dot{F} = f(F, M) \tag{13}$$

$$\dot{M} = g(F, M) \tag{14}$$

In the long–run equilibrium, the motion of foreign assets and the quantity of money comes to a standstill:

$$\dot{F} = \dot{M} = 0 \tag{15}$$

In real terms, once more, the long–run equilibrium is identical to that derived for flexible money wages.

Next we shall try to find out whether the long–run equilibrium will be stable. First catch a glimpse of the $\dot{F} = 0$ demarcation line. It can easily be seen that

$$\dot{F} = \beta\delta\mu K^{\alpha}(r^{\eta}\beta M/w)^{\beta} - \mu(F + K) \tag{16}$$

The proof follows the same lines as under slow money wages (for the special case I = 0). (16) implies $\partial\dot{F}/\partial F = -\mu < 0$. Then set (16) equal to zero and reshuffle terms $F = \beta\delta K^{\alpha}(r^{\eta}\beta M/w)^{\beta} - K$. Differentiate for M to furnish $dM/dF > 0$, thus the $\dot{F} = 0$ line is positively inclined, cf. figure 1. After that we shall ascertain the $\dot{M} = 0$ demarcation line. Substitute $N = r^{\eta}\beta M/w$ into (12):

$$\dot{M} = \kappa M - \beta\kappa r^{\eta}M^{2}/w\overline{N} \tag{17}$$

Moreover take the derivative $\partial\dot{M}/\partial M$ and evaluate it at the long–run equilibrium $M = w\overline{N}/\beta r^{\eta}$ to arrive at $\partial\dot{M}/\partial M < 0$. Then set (17) equal to zero, which yields $N = \overline{N}$. Finally combine this with $N = r^{\eta}\beta M/w$ to verify $M = w\overline{N}/\beta r^{\eta}$. That is why the $\dot{M} = 0$ line is horizontal. Assembling all component parts, figure 1 contains the phase diagram. As a consequence, the long–run equilibrium in fact is stable.

Imagine for example a monetary disturbance. At the beginning the economy is

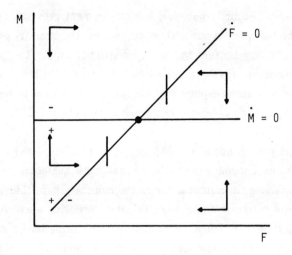

Figure 1
Dynamics of Foreign Assets and Money

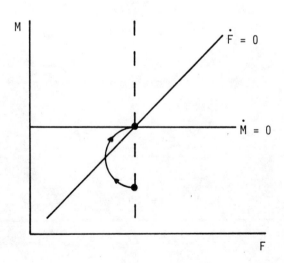

Figure 2
Monetary Shock and Slow Monetary Policy

in the stationary equilibrium. Above all, full employment prevails. Further let the foreign position be balanced. Against this background, the quantity of money diminishes autonomously, say because the money multiplier drops. The phase diagram reveals how the economy travels through time, cf. figure 2. In the short period, the ensuing appreciation worsens exports and output, so firms have to lay off workers. And the downswing of exports brings the current account into deficit.

In the medium period, due to the current account deficit, foreign debt piles up. And to overcome the unemployment, the central bank augments the quantity of money. Strictly speaking, it induces a rise in the monetary base. The accompanying depreciation improves exports and output, thereby alleviating unemployment. After a certain span of time, the deficit on current account turns into a surplus, which reverses the movement of foreign debt. In the long period, the economy will come back to full employment, and foreign debt will again disappear from the scene. To conclude, slow monetary policy is apt to restore full employment.

5. TWO COUNTRIES

5.1. OVERLAPPING GENERATIONS

In the present section, the analysis will be extended to include a second country. The investigation will be carried out within an overlapping generations model, providing a real analysis for flexible wages, cf. section 1.1. The long–run equilibrium can be written as a system of seven equations:

$$Y_i = K_i^{\alpha} \overline{N}_i^{\beta} \tag{1}$$

$$r = \alpha Y_i / K_i \tag{2}$$

$$F_i + K_i = \beta \delta_i Y_i \tag{3}$$

$$F_1 = -F_2 \tag{4}$$

Here the subscript i stands for the country in question. According to equation (1) we start from the premise that both countries agree in technology. Equation (2) states that the interest rate corresponds to the marginal product of capital. Under perfect capital mobility, the two interest rates coincide. By virtue of equation (3), actual wealth matches desired wealth. And equation (4) has it that the foreign assets of country 1 are identical to the foreign debt of country 2. α, β, δ_i and $\overline{N}_i$ are exogenous, while r, F_i, K_i and Y_i are endogenous. Further from (1) and (2) one can deduce that

$$Y_1/Y_2 = K_1/K_2 = \overline{N}_1/\overline{N}_2 \tag{5}$$

That is to say, the national allocation is uniform and governed by labour supply. It is independent, however, of the propensity to save δ_i.

Now contemplate the case $\overline{N}_1 \neq \overline{N}_2$ and $\delta_1 = \delta_2$. In other words, the countries differ in labour supply yet agree in time preference. In this case, the long–run equilibrium simplifies to a system of four equations:

$$Y_1 = K_1^{\alpha} \overline{N}_1^{\beta} \tag{6}$$

$$Y_2 = K_2^{\alpha} \overline{N}_2^{\beta} \tag{7}$$

$$Y_1/K_1 = Y_2/K_2 \tag{8}$$

$$K_1 + K_2 = \beta\delta(Y_1 + Y_2) \tag{9}$$

where K_1, K_2, Y_1 and Y_2 adjust themselves. It is helpful to define $Y = Y_1 + Y_2$, $K = K_1 + K_2$ and $\overline{N} = \overline{N}_1 + \overline{N}_2$. On that grounds, (6), (7) and (8) deliver $Y = K^{\alpha} \overline{N}^{\beta}$. And (9) can be reformulated as $K = \beta\delta Y$. Then combine the last two equations to reach $K = (\beta\delta)^{1/\beta} \overline{N}$ and, together with (8),

$$K_1 = (\beta\delta)^{1/\beta} \overline{N}_1 \tag{10}$$

What are the consequences of an increase in labour supply in country 1? Capital in country 1 springs up, whereas capital in country 2 does not stir. In full analogy, output in country 1 climbs, but output in country 2 remains unchanged. In addition, owing to $F_1 + K_1 = \beta\delta Y_1$, it holds $F_1 = 0$. Put another way, the foreign position will be balanced. To sum up, due to $\delta_1 = \delta_2$, the shock (in country 1) has no "external effects" (on country 2).

Next consider the reverse case $\delta_1 \neq \delta_2$ and $\overline{N}_1 = \overline{N}_2$. That means, the countries differ in time preference yet agree in labour supply. In this case, too, the long–run equilibrium can be described by a system of four equations:

$$Y_1 = K_1^{\alpha} \overline{N}_1^{\beta} \tag{11}$$

$$Y_2 = K_2^{\alpha} \overline{N}_2^{\beta} \tag{12}$$

$$Y_1/K_1 = Y_2/K_2 \tag{13}$$

$$K_1 + K_2 = \beta\delta_1 Y_1 + \beta\delta_2 Y_2 \tag{14}$$

where K_1, K_2, Y_1 and Y_2 adapt themselves. Insert $K_1 = K_2$ and $Y_1 = Y_2$ into (14) and regroup $2K_1 = \beta Y_1(\delta_1 + \delta_2)$. Besides combine this with (11) to gain:

$$K_1 = [\beta(\delta_1 + \delta_2)/2]^{1/\beta} \overline{N}_1 \tag{15}$$

How are the countries affected by a rise in the propensity to save of country 1? In both countries, the stock of capital will be elevated. And the same applies to output. In this sense, the impulse has positive external effects. Moreover, in conjunction with $F_1 + K_1 = \beta\delta_1 Y_1$, letting $\overline{N}_1 = \overline{N}_2 = 1$, it follows:

$$F_1 = [\beta(\delta_1 + \delta_2)/2]^{\alpha/\beta} \beta(\delta_1 - \delta_2)/2 \tag{16}$$

A boost in the propensity to save drives up foreign assets. Therefore the high–saving country will be a creditor.

5.2. FIXED MONEY WAGES

As a baseline, take the general model with fixed money wages, confer section 2.2. Beyond that we posit $I = 0$. For instance, have a look at a monetary expansion in country 1. Let us begin with the implications for country 1. Initially the economy is in the steady state. People suffer from unemployment. The current account balances, so foreign assets are constant. Suppose that domestic residents hold no foreign assets at the start. Under these circumstances, the quantity of money expands. In the short term, the ensuing depreciation advances exports and output, thereby bringing back full employment. The lift in exports moves the current account into surplus. In the intermediate term, the current account surplus builds up foreign assets round by round. Eventually the economy approaches a new steady state. Full employment still obtains. The current account balances again, hence foreign assets do no longer change. Properly speaking, the country has become a creditor.

Now turn to the spillover in country 2. Originally the economy is in the stationary equilibrium as well. The labour market clears. The current account breaks even, thus foreign assets are invariant. More exactly, imagine that foreign assets amount to zero. In the short term, the appreciation hampers exports and output, thus creating unemployment. Because of the drop in exports, the current account gets into deficit. In the intermediate term, the current account deficit adds to foreign debt period by period. In the end, the economy gravitates to a new stationary equilibrium. Some workers have lost their jobs. Once more, the current account breaks even, so foreign assets stop to pile up. Country 2 is a debtor, as opposed to country 1.

6. CAPITAL GAINS

At this juncture, capital gains on foreign assets will be incorporated into the analysis, occasioned e.g. by a depreciation. In doing this, we assume flexible money wages and no investment. As a point of reference, take the short—run equilibrium for flexible money wages in section 1.2., cf. equations (1) until (15). Let foreign assets F be denominated in foreign currency. Then eF denotes foreign assets in domestic currency and eF/p foreign assets in domestic goods. Correspondingly the interest inflow totals erF/p. In terms of domestic goods, the current account surplus is defined as $X + erF/p - Q$. Finally the current account surplus leads to the accumulation of foreign assets $e\dot{F}/p = X + erF/p - Q$. In domestic goods, actual wealth sums up to $A = eF/p + K$. And the income of domestic residents is made up of $Y + erF/p$.

The short—run equilibrium can be represented by a system of twelve equations:

$$Y = C + X - Q \tag{1}$$

$$Y = K^{\alpha}N^{\beta} \tag{2}$$

$$X = (ep^*/p)^{\theta} \tag{3}$$

$$Q = qC \tag{4}$$

$$e\dot{F}/p = X + erF/p - Q \tag{5}$$

$$Y + erF/p = C + S \tag{6}$$

$$S = \mu(A^* - A) \tag{7}$$

$$A^* = \beta\delta Y \tag{8}$$

$$A = eF/p + K \tag{9}$$

$$N = \overline{N} \tag{10}$$

$$w/p = \beta Y/N \tag{11}$$

$$M/p = Y/r^{\eta} \tag{12}$$

Here α, β, δ, η, θ, μ, p^*, q, r, F, K, M and $\overline{N}$ are exogenous, while e, p, w, A, A^*, C,

$\dot{F}$, N, Q, S, X and Y are endogenous.

Now we shall examine the stability of the long–run equilibrium. The comparison of (1) and (6) yields $S = X + er\dot{F}/p - Q$. Join this with (5) to see $e\dot{F}/p = S$. From (7), (8) and (9) one can infer the savings function $S = \mu(\beta\delta Y - eF/p - K)$. Substitute this into $e\dot{F}/p = S$ and rearrange $\dot{F} = \mu Z(\beta\delta Y - K) - \mu F$, where $Z = p/e$ by definition and $Y = K^\alpha \overline{N}^\beta = $ const by assumption. Then differentiate for F:

$$d\dot{F}/dF = \mu(\beta\delta Y - K)dZ/dF - \mu \tag{13}$$

Next we shall check the sign of the derivative. For that purpose, combine (6) with the savings function to attain the consumption function:

$$C = (1 - \beta\delta\mu)Y + erF/p + \mu(eF/p + K) \tag{14}$$

Accordingly, a depreciation raises both wealth and the interest inflow, thereby stimulating consumption. Further amalgamate (1) and (4) to reach $X = Y - (1 - q)C$. Letting be $\theta = p^* = 1$, equation (3) takes the shape $X = e/p$. In addition get rid of C by means of (14):

$$Z = \frac{1 + (1 - q)rF + (1 - q)\mu F}{[1 - (1 - q)(1 - \beta\delta\mu)]Y - (1 - q)\mu K} \tag{15}$$

Due to $X > 0$, the denominator is positive. Moreover differentiate (15) for F:

$$\frac{dZ}{dF} = \frac{(1 - q)(r + \mu)}{[1 - (1 - q)(1 - \beta\delta\mu)]Y - (1 - q)\mu K} \tag{16}$$

As a corrollary, $dZ/dF > 0$. Finally insert (16) into (13) and evaluate at the long–run equilibrium with $r = \alpha Y/K$. This involves a critical level of the interest rate:

$$r' = \frac{q + \alpha(1 - q)}{\beta\delta(1 - q)} \tag{17}$$

If $r \lessgtr r'$, then $d\dot{F}/dF \lessgtr 0$. That means, as long as the foreign interest rate is low, the long–run equilibrium will be stable. However, as soon as the foreign interest rate surpasses the critical level, the long–run equilibrium will be unstable. Confer this to a closed economy, where it is valid that $r = \alpha/\beta\delta$. In the neighbourhood of this interest rate, the long—run equilibrium will indeed be stable.

Over and above that, if there are no capital gains, the steady state is stable, as has been demonstrated in section 1.3. Similarly, if there were no interest flows, the steady state would be stable, too. Put differently, capital gains and interest flows are potential factors of instability. For a more detailed analysis of the underlying mechanism, have a look at the portfolio model in section 7. Last but not least, a critical remark is in place. Provided the variation in the exchange rate is only transitory, then capital gains as well are only transitory. As a consequence, they will at best leave a transitory impact. Or perhaps they will be ignored altogether.

7. PORTFOLIO MODEL

7.1. SHORT–RUN EQUILIBRIUM AND LONG–RUN EQUILIBRIUM

The investigation will be conducted within a simple model where domestic and foreign bonds are perfect substitutes. The wealth of domestic residents comprises three assets, money, domestic bonds and foreign bonds:

$$A = M + B + eF \tag{1}$$

Here A symbolizes the wealth of domestic residents, expressed in domestic currency. M stands for the stock of domestic money, in domestic currency. B is the stock of domestic bonds, in terms of domestic currency. By way of contrast, F is the stock of foreign bonds, in terms of foreign currency. e denotes the exchange rate, that is the price of foreign currency in terms of domestic currency. For that reason, eF is the stock of foreign bonds in terms of domestic currency. We postulate that the central bank fixes the stock of domestic money $M = $ const. The stock of domestic bonds is invariant, too $B = $ const. At least in the short run, the stock of foreign bonds is uniform as well $F = $ const.

We consider a small open economy, so the foreign interest rate is given $r^* = $ const. What is more, domestic and foreign bonds are perfect substitutes, hence the domestic interest rate coincides with the foreign interest rate $r = r^*$. Money demand changes in proportion to wealth $M^d = mA$. In equilibrium, the stock of money harmonizes with money demand $M = M^d$ or

$$M = mA \tag{2}$$

In full analogy, the demand for domestic and foreign bonds is proportional to wealth $B^d + eF^d = (1 - m)A$. In equilibrium, the stock of domestic and foreign bonds matches the demand for it $B + eF = B^d + eF^d$ or

$$B + eF = (1 - m)A \tag{3}$$

The portfolio equilibrium can be summed up by a system of three equations (1), (2) and (3). Apparently one of those equations is redundant. Henceforth the portfolio equilibrium will be indicated by equations (1) and (2). There B, F and M are exogenous, while e and A are endogenous.

In the next step, we shall install the full short—run equilibrium. Domestic output is determined by consumption, investment and exports minus imports $Y = C + I + X - Q$. For ease of exposition, let be $I = 0$. Exports are an increasing function of the exchange rate $X = e^{\theta}$ with elasticity θ. Imports, on the other hand, vary in proportion to consumption $Q = qC$. Domestic residents earn the interest rate r on foreign assets F, thus the interest inflow amounts to erF (in terms of domestic currency). The current account surplus can be defined as the excess of exports and interest inflow over imports $X + erF - Q$ (in domestic currency). And the current account surplus heaps up foreign assets $e\dot{F} = X + erF - Q$ (in domestic currency). By virtue of overlapping generations, desired wealth is proportionate to domestic income $A^* = aY$, cf. section 1.1. Savings are used to bridge the gap between desired and actual wealth round by round $S = \mu(A^* - A)$. Domestic income and interest inflow constitute the income of domestic residents $Y + erF$. It can be devoted, in turn, to consumption and savings $Y + erF = C + S$.

Taking all pieces together, the short—run equilibrium can be encapsulated in a system of nine equations:

$$Y = C + X - Q \tag{4}$$

$$X = e^{\theta} \tag{5}$$

$$Q = qC \tag{6}$$

$$e\dot{F} = X + erF - Q \tag{7}$$

$$A^* = aY \tag{8}$$

$$A = M + B + eF \tag{9}$$

$$S = \mu(A^* - A) \tag{10}$$

$$Y + erF = C + S \tag{11}$$

$$M = mA \tag{12}$$

Here θ, μ, a, m, q, r, B, F and M are given, whereas e, A, A^*, C, $\dot{F}$, Q, S, X and Y adjust themselves.

What are the main properties of the short–run equilibrium? To answer this question, substitute (9) into (12) and rearrange:

$$e = \frac{(1-m)M - mB}{mF} \tag{13}$$

A monetary expansion raises e, so domestic currency depreciates. Conversely, an addition to domestic bonds lowers e, hence domestic currency appreciates. And the same holds true for the accumulation of foreign assets. Further solve (12) for A = M/m. That means, a rise in the quantity of money brings about a proportionate rise in wealth. What is more, this outcome is independent of savings.

Now have a look at an open market operation. The central bank purchases domestic bonds in exchange for domestic money, thereby pushing up M and pulling down B. As a consequence, bond demand surpasses supply. The price of domestic bonds cannot go up, since this would reduce the domestic interest rate well below the foreign interest rate. The price of foreign bonds, on the other hand, is fixed for the small open economy. Instead, the exchange rate must climb. In this sense, the exchange rate is the price of foreign bonds. Accordingly, wealth mounts and thus money demand.

At this point we shall tackle the long–run equilibrium. The short–run equilibrium can be characterized by a single differential equation $\dot{F} = f(F)$. In the long–run equilibrium, foreign assets do no longer move $\dot{F} = 0$. Combine (4) and (11) to accomplish $e\dot{F} = S$. Due to $\dot{F} = 0$, we have S = 0. Insert this into (10), which yields $A^* = A$. Moreover pay attention to $A^* = aY$ and A = M/m to conclude:

$$Y = M/am \tag{14}$$

That is to say, income varies in proportion to the quantity of money. Finally, for later use, we shall derive consumption and exports. Starting from (11) and observing S = 0, state consumption explicitly C = Y + erF. Then eliminate eF with the help of (13) and note (14) to reach:

$$C = M/am + (1-m)rM/m - rB \tag{15}$$

Besides solve (4) for X, taking account of (6), to obtain X = Y – (1 – q)C. At last get rid of Y and C by means of (14) and (15):

$$X = qM/am - (1 - m)(1 - q)rM/m - (1 - q)rB \qquad (16)$$

What are the salient features of the long–run equilibrium? The current account balances, so foreign assets stop building up. Households do not save any more, hence wealth is uniform. And output remains unchanged. In other words, this is the steady state of a stationary economy.

7.2. STABILITY

First of all the comparison of $Y = C + X - Q$ and $Y + erF = C + S$ provides $e\dot{F}$ $= S$. Now put $A^* = aY$ and $A = M/m$ into $S = \mu(A^* - A)$ to deduce the savings function $S = \mu aY - \mu M/m$. Substitute this into $e\dot{F} = S$ and regroup:

$$\dot{F} = \mu aY/e - \mu M/em \qquad (1)$$

Next we shall eliminate Y and e. Let us begin with Y. Combine $Y + erF = C + S$ and $S = \mu aY - \mu M/m$ to get the consumption function $C = (1 - \mu a)Y + erF + \mu M/m$. Then place this together with $X = e^\theta$ and $Q = qC$ into $Y = C + X - Q$ and solve for Y:

$$Y = \frac{(1 - q)erF + (1 - q)\mu M/m + e^\theta}{1 - (1 - q)(1 - \mu a)} \qquad (2)$$

Owing to $\mu a + q > \mu aq$, the denominator of (2) is always positive. Further insert (2) into (1). Except for a factor of proportionality, one arrives at:

$$\dot{F} = ar(1 - q)F - qM/em + ae^{\theta - 1} \qquad (3)$$

A lift in F causes a drop in e. What does this imply for $\dot{F}$?

To solve this problem, take account of $e = [(1 - m)M - mB]/mF$ and reshuffle terms:

$$\dot{F} = ar(1 - q)F - \frac{qMF}{(1 - m)M - mB} + a\left[\frac{m}{(1 - m)M - mB}\right]^{1-\theta} F^{1-\theta} \qquad (4)$$

Then differentiate (4) for F and evaluate the derivative at the long–run equilibrium, cf. (16) in section 7.1. and $e^\theta = X$:

$$d\dot{F}/dF = \theta ar(1 - m)(1 - q)M - \theta amr(1 - q)B - \theta qM \qquad (5)$$

Subject to the condition

$$ar(1-q)[(1-m)M - mB] < qM \tag{6}$$

the derivative $d\dot{F}/dF$ will be negative. Therefore the sign of (5) hinges on a, m, q, r, B and M, irrespective of θ and μ. Phrased differently, there exists a critical level of the foreign interest rate r'. If $r \lessgtr r'$, then $d\dot{F}/dF \lessgtr 0$. In other words, if the foreign interest rate is low, the long–run equilibrium will be stable. However, if the foreign interest rate is high, the long–run equilibrium will be unstable.

By the way, if there were no interest flow, then r would be zero in (6). Correspondingly, the condition qM > 0 would always be fulfilled. On that grounds, the long–run equilibrium would be stable in any case. Thus the interest flow is a potential factor of instability.

7.3. MONETARY SHOCK

Originally the economy is in the steady state. The current account balances, so foreign assets are constant. In this situation, the quantity of money increases spontaneously. In the short term, domestic currency depreciates, which enhances exports and output. In the intermediate term, by virtue of the current account surplus, foreign assets pile up. The rise in foreign assets induces a fall in the exchange rate such that eF is invariant, hence wealth does not respond. The appreciation just mentioned depresses exports and output. And the cut in exports diminishes the current account surplus. Figure 1 shows the time path of output for the stable case.

Beyond that we shall try to make sense of the stability condition. Essentially it requires that $\dot{F}$ comes down as F goes up. As a baseline, regard the current account equation $e\dot{F} = X + erF - Q$. That means, the current account surplus is the excess of exports and interest inflow over imports, expressed in domestic currency. Now it proves useful to restate this in terms of foreign currency $\dot{F} = X/e + rF - Q/e$. How is $\dot{F}$ affected by a lift in F? Properly speaking, there are three channels of transmission. First the accumulation of foreign assets lowers the exchange rate and exports. Letting X/e be uniform, this has no influence on $\dot{F}$. Second the accumulation of foreign assets raises the interest inflow and thus $\dot{F}$. Third the accumulation of foreign assets reduces the exchange rate, exports, output, consumption and imports. Letting the decline in imports be smaller than the decline in exports, Q/e will expand and $\dot{F}$ will contract. What is the net effect? It depends on the interest inflow and on the foreign interest rate. When the foreign interest rate is low, a rise in F leads to a fall in $\dot{F}$, so the long–term equilibrium will be stable. Conversely, when the foreign interest rate is high, a rise in F occasions a rise in $\dot{F}$, so the long–term equilibrium will be unstable.

In foreign currency, the mechanism works like this. Let us start with a current account surplus that contributes to the buildup of foreign assets. This boosts the interest inflow and imports, but leaves no impact on exports. As a consequence, the current account surplus may shrink or swell. Accordingly, the steady state will be stable or unstable.

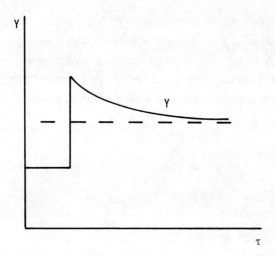

Figure 1
Output (Stable Case)

At last contemplate the long—term effects of the monetary expansion for the unstable case. Eventually foreign assets will tend to explode, thereby driving the exchange rate down to zero. In domestic currency, this squeezes exports down to zero as well. For that reason, output will become very small. As a result, this is the vicious circle of current account surplus, foreign assets and interest inflow (in terms of foreign currency).

Chapter II. Economy with Public Sector

Here the basic model will be extended to include the public sector. The government levies taxes and raises loans in order to finance public consumption and the interest payments on public debt. Public borrowing in turn adds to public debt. The analysis will be implemented within an IS–LM model characterized by the dynamics of public debt, foreign assets, private capital and money wages.

As a frame of reference, in section 1, we shall install the overlapping generations model. Then, in sections 2 until 4, we shall consider an IS–LM model, studying the dynamic consequences of macroeconomic shocks. There it proves useful to distinguish between flexible, fixed and slow money wages. As an exception, in section 5, we shall assume continuous budget balance. Over and above that, in sections 6 until 8, we shall discuss monetary and fiscal policy as dynamic instruments to overcome macroeconomic shocks. In section 9, two separate countries will be incorporated. Finally, in section 10, we shall deal with the portfolio model.

1. OVERLAPPING GENERATIONS

The investigation will be conducted within an overlapping generations model without bequests (Diamond 1965). The current section offers the real analysis of a stationary economy. The purpose is to deliver a microfoundation for (the long–run equilibrium in) the extended model.

Let labour supply be given exogenously $\overline{N}$ = const. Wages are flexible so as to adapt labour demand N to labour supply:

$$N = \overline{N} \tag{1}$$

Put another way, full employment prevails forever. Businesses manufacture a single product Y by making use of capital K and labour N. Properly speaking, N denotes the number of active workers. For the sake of convenience, assume a Cobb–Douglas technology:

$$Y = K^{\alpha} N^{\beta} \tag{2}$$

with $\alpha > 0$, $\beta > 0$ and $\alpha + \beta = 1$. Output Y can be dedicated to private consumption C, private investment I, public consumption G, exports X and imports Q:

$$Y = C + I + G + X - Q \tag{3}$$

Consider a small open economy with perfect capital mobility, hence the domestic interest rate agrees with the foreign interest rate $r = r^* $ = const. Businesses maximize profits Π under perfect competition:

$$\Pi = Y - rK - wN \tag{4}$$

Differentiate (4) for K and set the derivative equal to zero:

$$r = \frac{\partial Y}{\partial K} = \frac{\alpha Y}{K} \tag{5}$$

That is to say, the marginal product of capital corresponds to the interest rate. Analogously, one obtains:

$$w = \frac{\partial Y}{\partial N} = \frac{\beta Y}{N} \tag{6}$$

In other words, the wage rate agrees with the marginal product of labour.

The government collects an income tax and raises loans in order to finance both public consumption and the interest payments on public debt. The government purchases a specified volume of goods:

$$G = \text{const} \tag{7}$$

D stands for public debt owed by the government to the private sector. The government pays the interest rate r on public debt D, so public interest amounts to rD. Moreover, the government imposes a tax T at the flat rate t = const on factor income Y and on debt income rD:

$$T = t(Y + rD) \tag{8}$$

The budget deficit can be defined as the excess of public consumption and public interest over tax earnings:

$$B = G + rD - T \tag{9}$$

The government covers the budget deficit by borrowing from the private sector. The budget deficit, in turn, contributes to the accumulation of public debt:

$$D_{+1} = D + B \tag{10}$$

In the long-run equilibrium, public debt does no longer move $D_{+1} = D$, so the budget will be balanced:

$$B = 0 \tag{11}$$

That is why the government budget constraint (9) simplifies to:

$$G + rD = t(Y + rD) \tag{12}$$

Domestic residents earn the net interest rate $(1 - t)r$ on foreign assets F, thus the interest inflow totals $(1 - t)rF$. The underlying premise is that foreign assets are taxed abroad. The current account surplus equals exports plus interest inflow minus imports:

$$E = X + (1 - t)rF - Q \tag{13}$$

Foreign assets and the current account surplus this period provide foreign assets next period:

$$F_{+1} = F + E \tag{14}$$

In the long–run equilibrium, foreign assets do not build up any more $F_{+1} = F$, hence the current account balances:

$$E = 0 \tag{15}$$

The individual lifecycle is composed of two periods, of the working period and of the retirement period. During the working period, the individual receives labour income, which he partly consumes and partly saves. The savings are used to buy government bonds, foreign bonds and private domestic bonds. During the retirement period, the individual earns interest on the bonds and sells the bonds altogether. The proceeds are entirely consumed, no bequests are left.

The utility u of the representative individual depends on private consumption per head in the working period c^1 and on private consumption per head in the retirement period c^2. Take a logarithmic utility function:

$$u = \gamma \log c^1 + \delta \log c^2 \tag{16}$$

with $\gamma > 0$, $\delta > 0$ and $\gamma + \delta = 1$. We postulate that public consumption does not affect intertemporal allocation. That means, public consumption does not enter the utility function explicitly.

The budget constraint of the representative individual covers the whole lifecycle.

$(1 - t)w$ is net labour income in the working period and $(1 - t)w - c^1$ are private savings in the working period. The individual earns the net rate of interest $(1 - t)r$ on private savings, so private consumption in the retirement period is $[(1 - t)w - c^1]\ [1 + (1 - t)r] = c^2$. As a consequence, the individual budget constraint can be stated as:

$$c^1 + \frac{c^2}{1 + (1 - t)r} = (1 - t)w \tag{17}$$

The individual chooses present and future consumption so as to maximize utility subject to its budget constraint. The evaluation of the Lagrange function yields private consumption per head in the working period:

$$c^1 = \gamma(1 - t)w \tag{18}$$

Net labour income minus private consumption per head gives private savings per head $a = (1 - t)w - c^1$ or

$$a = \delta(1 - t)w \tag{19}$$

The private savings of the active generation amount to $A = aN$. Observe (19) and (6) to arrive at:

$$A = \beta\delta(1 - t)Y \tag{20}$$

The private savings of the young generation serve to finance public debt, foreign assets and private capital of the subsequent period:

$$D_{+1} + F_{+1} + K_{+1} = A \tag{21}$$

In the long-run equilibrium, public debt, foreign assets and private capital are invariant $D_{+1} = D$, $F_{+1} = F$ and $K_{+1} = K$. Insert this together with (20) into (21) to reach:

$$D + F + K = \beta\delta(1 - t)Y \tag{22}$$

Besides, private investment augments the stock of capital:

$$K_{+1} = K + I \tag{23}$$

In the steady state, the stock of capital is uniform, so firms do not invest:

$$I = 0 \tag{24}$$

To summarize, the long—run equilibrium can be captured by a system of four equations:

$$Y = K^\alpha \overline{N}^\beta \tag{25}$$

$$r = \alpha Y/K \tag{26}$$

$$G + rD = t\,(Y + rD) \tag{27}$$

$$D + F + K = \beta\delta(1-t)Y \tag{28}$$

Here α, β, δ, r, t, G and $\overline{N}$ are fixed, while D, F, K and Y adjust themselves appropriately.

What are the major attributes of the long—run equilibrium? The labour market clears. Both the budget and the current account balance, thus public debt and foreign assets stay put. Businesses abstain from investment, hence private capital is constant. And labour supply is given, so output does not change. Once more this is the steady state of a stationary economy.

Finally the system (25) until (28) will be solved for the endogenous variables. Combine (25) and (26) to get:

$$K = (\alpha/r)^{1/\beta}\,\overline{N} \tag{29}$$

$$Y = (\alpha/r)^{\alpha/\beta}\,\overline{N} \tag{30}$$

That is to say, public consumption and the tax rate have no influence on capital and output. Further eliminate Y in (27) with the help of (30) and rearrange:

$$D = \frac{t(\alpha/r)^{\alpha/\beta}\,\overline{N} - G}{(1 - t)\,r} \tag{31}$$

As a result, an increase in public consumption reduces public debt, which seems to be somewhat like a paradox. Therefore one may suspect that the long–run equilibrium will be unstable.

2. FLEXIBLE MONEY WAGES

2.1. SHORT–RUN EQUILIBRIUM AND LONG–RUN EQUILIBRIUM

The investigation will be performed within the following setting. Labour supply is given exogenously $\overline{N}$ = const. Money wages are flexible, so labour demand corresponds to labour supply $N = \overline{N}$. Firms employ capital K and labour N to produce a homogeneous commodity Y. Let technology be of the Cobb–Douglas type $Y = K^{\alpha}N^{\beta}$ with $\alpha + \beta = 1$. Output is determined by private consumption, private investment, public consumption, exports and imports $Y = C + I + G + X - Q$. Regard a small open economy with perfect capital mobility, hence the domestic interest rate agrees with the foreign interest rate $r = r^* =$ const. Firms maximize profits $\Pi = pY - prK - wN$ under perfect competition, thus the marginal product of capital harmonizes with the interest rate $r = \partial Y/\partial K = \alpha Y/K$. From this one can deduce the desired stock of capital $K^* = \alpha Y/r$. Similarly, the real wage rate accords with the marginal product of labour $w/p = \partial Y/\partial N = \beta Y/N$.

Now we come to dynamics, let us begin with private investment. Private investment serves to fill the gap between desired capital K^* and actual capital K round by round $I = \lambda(K^* - K)$. Here $0 < \lambda < 1$ denotes the speed of adjustment. Of course, private investment adds to the stock of private capital $\dot{K} = I$. The second point refers to government budget dynamics. The government fixes public consumption G = const. It pays the interest rate r on public debt D, so public interest amounts to rD. The government levies a proportionate tax on factor income and debt income $T = t(Y + rD)$. The difference between public expenditures and tax revenue is called budget deficit $G + rD - T$. The budget deficit in turn leads to the growth of public debt $\dot{D} = G + rD - T$.

Next have a look at current account dynamics. Exports are positively correlated with the real exchange rate $X = (ep^*/p)^{\theta}$, and imports move in proportion to private consumption $Q = qC$. Domestic residents earn the net interest rate $(1 - t)r$ on foreign assets F, hence the interest inflow totals $(1 - t)rF$. This rests on the assumption that foreign assets are taxed abroad. Exports plus interest inflow minus imports make up the current account surplus $E = X + (1 - t)rF - Q$. The current account surplus in turn contributes to the accumulation of foreign assets $\dot{F} = E$. The last point relates to private savings dynamics. Due to overlapping generations, desired wealth is proportionate to domestic income $A^* = \beta\delta(1-t)Y$, cf. section 1. Actual wealth, on the other hand, encompasses public debt, foreign assets and private capital $A = D + F + K$. Private savings are used to overcome the discrepancy between desired and actual wealth period by period $S = \mu(A^* - A)$, where $0 < \mu < 1$ symbolizes the velocity of adaptation. Evidently private savings augment the stock of private wealth $\dot{A} = S$. The income of domestic residents consists of domestic income, public interest and the interest inflow $Y + rD + (1-t)rF$. It can be devoted to private consumption, private savings and tax payments $Y + rD + (1-t)rF = C + S + T$.

Finally a few words will be said on the money market. The real demand for money is an increasing function of income and a declining function of the interest rate $L = Y/r^{\eta}$. The central bank controls the nominal quantity of money $M = $ const. In equilibrium, the real supply of money conforms with the real demand for it $M/p = Y/r^{\eta}$.

In summary, the short–run equilibrium can be represented by a system of seventeen equations:

$$Y = C + I + G + X - Q \tag{1}$$

$$Y = K^{\alpha}N^{\beta} \tag{2}$$

$$K^* = \alpha Y/r \tag{3}$$

$$I = \lambda(K^* - K) \tag{4}$$

$$\dot{K} = I \tag{5}$$

$$T = t(Y + rD) \tag{6}$$

$$\dot{D} = G + rD - T \tag{7}$$

$$X = (ep^*/p)^{\theta} \tag{8}$$

$$Q = qC \tag{9}$$

$$\dot{F} = X + (1-t)rF - Q \tag{10}$$

$$Y + rD + (1-t)rF = C + S + T \tag{11}$$

$$S = \mu(A^* - A) \tag{12}$$

$$A^* = \beta\delta(1-t)Y \tag{13}$$

$$A = D + F + K \tag{14}$$

$$N = \overline{N} \tag{15}$$

$$w/p = \beta Y/N \tag{16}$$

$$M/p = Y/r^\eta \tag{17}$$

Here α, β, δ, η, θ, λ, μ, p^*, q, r, t, D, F, G, K, M and $\overline{N}$ are exogenous, while e, p, w, A, A^*, C, $\dot{D}$, $\dot{F}$, I, K^*, $\dot{K}$, N, Q, S, T, X and Y are endogenous.

The short–run equilibrium can be compressed to a system of three differential equations:

$$\dot{D} = f(D, F, K) \tag{18}$$

$$\dot{F} = g(D, F, K) \tag{19}$$

$$\dot{K} = h(D, F, K) \tag{20}$$

In the long–run equilibrium, public debt, foreign assets and private capital do no longer move:

$$\dot{D} = \dot{F} = \dot{K} = 0 \tag{21}$$

For the remainder of this section, the long–run equilibrium will be sketched out briefly. The comparison of (1) and (11) yields $\dot{D} + \dot{F} + \dot{K} = S$. That means, budget deficit, current account surplus and private investment add up to private savings. Owing to (21) it is valid that S = 0. Substitute this into (12) to gain $A = A^*$. In conjunction with (13) and (14) this furnishes $D + F + K = \beta\delta(1-t)Y$. Then combine (5) and (21) to see I = 0 and, together with (4), $K = K^*$. Hence (3) implies $K = \alpha Y/r$ and $r = \alpha Y/K$. Therefore the long–run equilibrium can be written as a system of four equations:

$$Y = K^\alpha \overline{N}^\beta \qquad (22)$$

$$r = \alpha Y/K \qquad (23)$$

$$G + rD = t(Y + rD) \qquad (24)$$

$$D + F + K = \beta\delta(1-t)Y \qquad (25)$$

As a corollary, the long–run equilibrium is identical to that derived for overlapping generations, cf. (25) until (28) in section 1. In full analogy, one obtains $Y = (\alpha/r)^{\alpha/\beta}\,\overline{N}$ and $K = (\alpha/r)^{1/\beta}\,\overline{N}$.

2.2. STABILITY AND SHOCK

In doing the stability analysis, we postulate $I = 0$ and $K = $ const. For that reason, the short–run equilibrium simplifies to:

$$Y = C + G + X - Q \tag{1}$$

$$Y = K^{\alpha} N^{\beta} \tag{2}$$

$$T = t(Y + rD) \tag{3}$$

$$\dot{D} = G + rD - T \tag{4}$$

$$X = (ep^*/p)^{\theta} \tag{5}$$

$$Q = qC \tag{6}$$

$$\dot{F} = X + (1 - t)rF - Q \tag{7}$$

$$Y + rD + (1 - t)rF = C + S + T \tag{8}$$

$$S = \mu(A^* - A) \tag{9}$$

$$A^* = \beta\delta(1 - t)Y \tag{10}$$

$$A = D + F + K \tag{11}$$

$$N = \overline{N} \tag{12}$$

$$w/p = \beta Y/N \tag{13}$$

$$M/p = Y/r^{\eta} \tag{14}$$

Here e, p, w, A, A^*, C, $\dot{D}$, $\dot{F}$, N, Q, S, T, X and Y accommodate suitably.

In this special case, the short–run equilibrium can be condensed to a system of two differential equations $\dot{D} = f(D, F)$ and $\dot{F} = g(D, F)$. In the long–run equilibrium, the motion of public debt and foreign assets comes to a halt $\dot{D} = \dot{F} = 0$. In the steady state, output is uniform since private capital and labour supply are uniform, as can be learned from $Y = K^{\alpha} \overline{N}^{\beta}$.

Now we shall try to find out the $\dot{D} = 0$ demarcation line. Merge (3) and (4) to conclude:

$$\dot{D} = G + (1-t)rD - tY \tag{15}$$

From this one can infer $\partial\dot{D}/\partial D = (1-t)\,r > 0$. Then set (15) equal to zero and solve for $D = (tY - G)/(1-t)r$. As a consequence, the $\dot{D} = 0$ line is vertical, cf. figure 1. Next we shall explore the $\dot{F} = 0$ demarcation line. The comparison of (1) and (8) provides $\dot{F} = S - \dot{D}$. Insert here the saving function $S = \beta\delta\mu(1-t)Y - \mu(D + F + K)$ as well as (15) and regroup:

$$\dot{F} = \beta\delta\mu(1-t)Y - \mu(D + F + K) - G - (1-t)rD + tY \tag{16}$$

This involves $\partial\dot{F}/\partial F = -\mu < 0$. Likewise set (16) equal to zero and differentiate adequately $dF/dD = -(\mu + (1-t)r)/\mu < 0$. Put another way, the $\dot{F} = 0$ line is downward sloping, cf. figure 1.

Assembling all component parts, figure 1 contains the phase diagram. As a fundamental result, the long–run equilibrium proves to be unstable. This is in sharp contrast to the conclusions drawn for the basic model where the long–run equilibrium turned out to be stable. In other words, the public sector creates long–run instability.

At this juncture, we shall keep track of the process of adjustment induced by a fiscal shock. Initially the economy is in the steady state. The budget and the current account balance, so public debt and foreign assets are constant. More precisely, let public debt and foreign assets be zero at the start. Under these circumstances, the government increases its purchases of goods and services. In the phase diagram, both demarcation lines shift to the left, cf. figure 2. In the short term, domestic currency appreciates, which hinders exports. On balance, output remains unaffected. The rise in public consumption brings the budget into deficit, and the ensuing fall in exports brings the current account into deficit. Strictly speaking, the current account deficit is equivalent to the budget deficit. That is to say, indirectly the government borrows abroad.

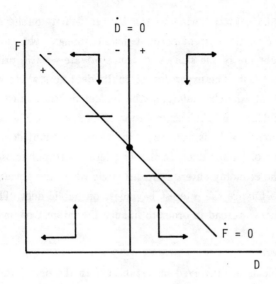

Figure 1
Dynamics of Public Debt and Foreign Assets

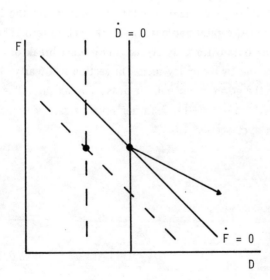

Figure 2
Fiscal Shock

In the intermediate term, owing to the budget deficit, public debt begins to grow. Similarly, due to the current account deficit, foreign debt builds up. Public debt and foreign debt are of the same size, hence private wealth, private consumption and output hold fast. The expansion of public debt goes along with an expansion of public interest, thereby enlarging the budget deficit, which speeds up the expansion of public debt. And the accumulation of foreign debt is accompanied by a swelling of interest outflow. This aggravates the current account deficit and reinforces the accumulation of foreign debt. In the long term, both public and foreign debt tend to explode. The economy enters a vicious circle where the government borrows at home in order to finance the interest payments on public debt. That is why domestic residents borrow abroad in order to finance the interest payments on foreign debt.

Now what problems are involved in instability? In the model there is no hardship: Output, private consumption and private wealth are stable, only public and foreign debt are unstable. The underlying reason is that the budget deficit is financed by raising loans abroad. In the small open economy, the interest rate does not climb in response. Therefore, no crowding out of private investment does occur. But in the real world, as public and foreign debt proliferate without bounds, the open economy will not be small any longer. Instead, this drives up the foreign interest rate, thus curbing private investment, capital and output. As the foreign interest rate grows without limits, capital and output shrink back to zero. That means there will be fatal crowding out. Ultimately the economy must break down. For a more detailed analysis, see the two–country model in section 9. Clearly this is not optimal. Sooner or later the government must increase the tax rate. The later this happens, the larger the increase must be. A rather simple strategy would be to balance the budget at all times, cf. section 5.

3. FIXED MONEY WAGES

3.1. SHORT–RUN EQUILIBRIUM, LONG–RUN EQUILIBRIUM AND STABILITY

As a point of departure take the short–run equilibrium under flexible money wages, cf. (1) until (17) in section 2.1. The sole distinction is that here money wages are exogenous while labour demand becomes endogenous. Generally the economy will suffer from underemployment (or overemployment), $N = \bar{N}$ does no longer apply. For ease of exposition let be $I = 0$, so K is invariant.

Accordingly the short–run equilibrium can be written as a system of thirteen equations:

$$Y = C + G + X - Q \tag{1}$$

$$Y = K^{\alpha} N^{\beta} \tag{2}$$

$$T = t(Y + rD) \tag{3}$$

$$\dot{D} = G + rD - T \tag{4}$$

$$X = (ep^*/p)^{\theta} \tag{5}$$

$$Q = qC \tag{6}$$

$$\dot{F} = X + (1 - t)rF - Q \tag{7}$$

$$Y + rD + (1 - t)rF = C + S + T \tag{8}$$

$$S = \mu(A^* - A) \tag{9}$$

$$A^* = \beta\delta(1 - t)Y \tag{10}$$

$$A = D + F + K \tag{11}$$

$$w/p = \beta Y/N \tag{12}$$

$$M/p = Y/r^{\eta} \tag{13}$$

In this case α, β, δ, η, θ, μ, p^*, q, r, t, w, D, F, G, K and M are given, whereas e, p, A, A^*, C, $\dot{D}$, $\dot{F}$, N, Q, S, T, X and Y adapt themselves.

How does the short—run equilibrium look like? First solve (12) for $N = \beta pY/w$. Then get rid of pY by means of (13) to accomplish $N = r^{\eta}\beta M/w$. That is to say, labour demand is constant, except for a one—time jump together with the quantity of money. Finally substitute this into (2) to arrive at $Y = K^{\alpha}(r^{\eta}\beta M/w)^{\beta}$. In full analogy, output remains unchanged. The short—run equilibrium can be reformulated as a system of two differential equations $\dot{D} = f(D, F)$ and $\dot{F} = g(D, F)$. In the long—run equilibrium, public and foreign debt cease to move $\dot{D} = \dot{F} = 0$.

Next we shall probe into stability. Let us begin with the $\dot{D} = 0$ demarcation line. Insert (3) into (4) and reshuffle:

$$\dot{D} = G + (1-t)rD - tY \tag{14}$$

Then differentiate for D to verify $\partial\dot{D}/\partial D = (1-t)r > 0$. Besides set (14) equal to zero and reshuffle $D = (tY - G)/(1-t)r$. In other words, public debt is uniform, hence the $\dot{D} = 0$ line is vertical, cf figure 1 in section 2.2. Moreover consider the $\dot{F} = 0$ demarcation line. The evaluation of (1) and (8) delivers $\dot{F} = S - D$. Pay attention to the savings function $S = \beta\delta\mu(1-t)Y - \mu(D + F + K)$ as well as to (14):

$$\dot{F} = \beta\delta\mu(1-t)Y - \mu(D + F + K) - G - (1-t)rD + tY \tag{15}$$

Further take the derivative $\partial\dot{F}/\partial F = -\mu < 0$. Similarly set (15) equal to zero, solve for F and differentiate for D to see $dF/dD = -[\mu + (1-t)r]/\mu < 0$. Thus the $\dot{F} = 0$ line is downward sloping.

The phase diagram is isomorphic to that presented in section 2.2. As a principal result, the long—run equilibrium will be unstable. This is in remarkable opposition to the basic model, where the long—run equilibrium was stable. Put another way, the public sector creates long—run instability.

3.2. MONETARY SHOCK

Originally the economy rests in the steady state. In particular, the budget and the current account balance. Over and above that, at the start, let the labour market clear, and let there be neither public nor foreign debt. Against this background, the quantity of money diminishes spontaneously. In the phase diagram, both demarcation lines travel to the left, cf. figure 1. In the short term, the subsequent appreciation curtails exports and output, thereby causing unemployment. The decline in exports brings the current account into deficit. And the reduction in income is associated with a reduction in tax earnings, which moves the budget into deficit. By virtue of the savings function, private savings come down since income falls.

In the intermediate term, owing to the budget deficit, public debt begins to grow. Due to the current account deficit, foreign debt builds up. And the negative savings lower private wealth round by round. Beyond that, the cut in private wealth leads to a cut in private consumption. Therefore domestic currency depreciates, so exports recover. The net effect is that output stays put. The expansion of public debt entails an expansion of public interest. This in turn enhances the budget deficit, thus amplifying the growth of public debt. Likewise the accumulation of foreign debt gives rise to a surging interest outflow. This augments the current account deficit and accelerates the heaping up of foreign debt. Eventually public and foreign debt tend to explode. And the economy is still subject to unemployment.

In addition, catch a glimpse of the time paths generated by the monetary shock. Figure 2 portrays the jump in output, and the jump in labour demand looks very similar. The interaction of private savings and private wealth reminds one of the basic model. The same holds true for the trajectory of private consumption. The time path of the exchange rate divides into two phases, cf. figure 3. At first the exchange rate drops sharply, later on recuperating to a certain degree. That is to say, the exchange rate overshoots in the short term. Figure 4 plots the trajectory of exports, which distinctly reflects the accommodation of the exchange rate.

At this stage, one may object that in the real world the proliferation of foreign debt pushes up the foreign interest rate. In the short term, the capital inflow lessens, thereby depreciating domestic currency and advancing exports. On the other hand, the concomitant increase in the domestic interest rate hampers private investment.

106

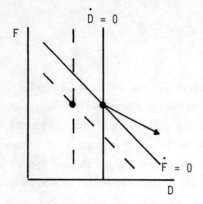

Figure 1
Monetary Shock

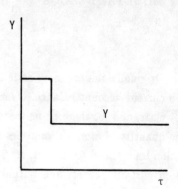

Figure 2
Income

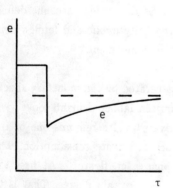

Figure 3
Exchange Rate

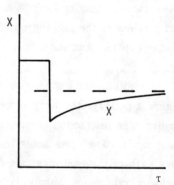

Figure 4
Exports

On balance, aggregate demand and output improve, which alleviates unemployment. In the intermediate term, the negative investment dismantles the stock of capital period by period. This in turn depresses output. In the long term, as foreign debt grows without limits, the foreign interest rate blows up, thus squeezing capital and output down to zero.

4. SLOW MONEY WAGES

The rate of change of money wages is a decreasing function of the rate of unemployment. As compared to flexible money wages, $\dot{w} = \epsilon w(N/\overline{N} - 1)$ takes the place of $N = \overline{N}$. Apart from this, we follow the same avenue as before.

The temporary equilibrium can be captured by a system of four differential equations:

$$\dot{w} = f(w, D, F, K) \tag{1}$$

$$\dot{D} = g(w, D, F, K) \tag{2}$$

$$\dot{F} = h(w, D, F, K) \tag{3}$$

$$\dot{K} = j(w, D, F, K) \tag{4}$$

In the permanent equilibrium, money wages, public debt, foreign assets and private capital stop adjusting:

$$\dot{w} = \dot{D} = \dot{F} = \dot{K} = 0 \tag{5}$$

As an implication, the permanent equilibrium for slow money wages coincides with the permanent equilibrium for flexible money wages. What is more, the permanent equilibrium for slow money wages will be unstable. This underlines the importance of the results obtained for flexible and fixed money wages.

5. CONTINUOUS BUDGET BALANCE

In the preceding sections, public consumption and the tax rate were assumed to be given. The excess of government expenditures over tax receipts adds to public debt $\dot{D} = G + rD - T$. And the government levies a tax on both factor income and debt income $T = t(Y + rD)$. In the current section, instead, we shall postulate continuous budget balance. As a response to a shock, the government continuously adjusts public consumption so as to always balance the budget. $G = T = tY$ implies $B = 0$ and $D = 0$. Under this alternative strategy, public debt does not occur. For the sake of convenience, consider slow money wages and neglect private investment.

The short—run equilibrium can be set out as a system of fourteen equations:

$$Y = C + G + X - Q \tag{1}$$

$$Y = K^{\alpha}N^{\beta} \tag{2}$$

$$T = tY \tag{3}$$

$$G = T \tag{4}$$

$$X = (ep^*/p)^{\theta} \tag{5}$$

$$Q = qC \tag{6}$$

$$\dot{F} = X + (1-t)rF - Q \tag{7}$$

$$Y + (1-t)rF = C + S + T \tag{8}$$

$$S = \mu(A^* - A) \tag{9}$$

$$A^* = \beta\delta(1-t)Y \tag{10}$$

$$A = F + K \tag{11}$$

$$\dot{w} = \epsilon w(N/\overline{N} - 1) \tag{12}$$

$$w/p = \beta Y/N \tag{13}$$

$$M/p = Y/r^{\eta} \tag{14}$$

Here α, β, δ, η, θ, μ, p^*, q, r, t, w, F, K, M and $\overline{N}$ are exogenous, while e, p, $\dot{w}$, A,

A^*, C, $\dot{F}$, G, N, Q, S, T, X and Y are endogenous. In this version, the tax rate is fixed, whereas public consumption adapts itself. In place of this, one could imagine that public consumption were constant and the tax rate were variable. The system (1) until (14) is structurally identical to that derived for an economy without public sector, cf (1) until (12) in section 3.1. As a consequence, the long—run equilibrium turns out to be stable.

Take for instance a monetary contraction. In the short run, the shock damages output. On account of the fall in tax earnings, the government must lower its purchases of goods and services. Then, in the medium run, output rallies. Because of the rise in tax earnings, the government has to lift its purchases. The post—shock steady state agrees with the pre—shock steady state, at least in real terms.

This outcome is in clear contradistinction to an economy with budget deficits, where the long—run equilibrium proved to be unstable. In summary, continuous budget balance restores long—run stability. The other way round, public debt creates long—run instability.

6. MONETARY POLICY

In this section, we assume flexible monetary policy. As a response to a shock, the central bank continuously adjusts the quantity of money so as to maintain full employment at all times. Accordingly, there is no reason why money wages should change. Can this strategy be sustained? In doing the analysis, we leave the premise of continuous budget balance. Besides we posit slow money wages. The short–run equilibrium coincides with that obtained for flexible money wages, cf (1) until (17) in section 2.1. The only difference is that here the quantity of money becomes endogenous, while money wages get exogenous. As a major result, the long–run equilibrium will be unstable.

For example have a look at an interest shock. Originally the economy is in the stationary equilibrium. Especially, all workers have got a job. At the start, let domestic residents hold neither government bonds nor foreign bonds. In this situation, the foreign interest rate goes up. In the short term, capital flows out, which depreciates domestic currency, so exports climb. Further the domestic interest rate comes up, thereby discouraging private investment. The net effect is to raise aggregate demand and output, hence overemployment emerges. Instantaneously, in order to avoid this, the central bank switches to a tight monetary policy. The ensuing appreciation lowers exports, aggregate demand and output. In the short term equilibrium, the labour market clears, and the government budget is balanced. However, the current account registers a surplus, and private investment is negative.

In the intermediate term, owing to the negative investment, the stock of capital dwindles away. Moreover the diminution in capital leads to a diminution in full–employment output $\overline{Y} = K^{\alpha} \overline{N}^{\beta}$. This in turn cuts back tax revenue, thus the budget gets into deficit. And the budget deficit makes for the growth of public debt. In the long term, public debt tends to explode. To conclude, monetary policy succeeds in always keeping up full employment. On the other hand, the proliferation of public debt is not feasible in the long term.

How does flexible monetary policy perform in general? Under a monetary disturbance or a wage impulse, the long–term equilibrium will be stable. Conversely, under an interest shock, a labour supply shock or a savings shock, the long–term equilibrium will be unstable, as opposed to an economy without public sector, where the long—term equilibrium was stable, cf. section 4.

7. FISCAL POLICY

In the present section, we are concerned with flexible fiscal policy. As a response to a shock, the government continuously adjusts public consumption so as to maintain full employment at all times. Correspondingly, there is no reason why money wages should vary. Can this strategy be sustained? In answering this question, we suppose that money wages are slow.

Apparently, the short–run equilibrium harmonizes with that established for flexible money wages, cf. (1) until (17) in section 2.1. The sole departure is that here public consumption becomes endogenous, while money wages get exogenous. As a finding, the long–run equilibrium will be unstable. In addition, a more profound difficulty is associated with fiscal policy. An increase in public consumption appreciates domestic currency, in this way supplanting exports. On balance, fiscal policy leaves no impact on output and employment. In other words, fiscal policy proves to be ineffective, as is well known.

8. MONETARY POLICY WITH CONTINUOUS BUDGET BALANCE

To begin with, we shall present an overview of the conclusions drawn in the foregoing sections. First, under slow money wages, the economy will suffer from both unemployment and long–run instability, cf. section 4. Second, continuous budget balance restores long–run stability. On the other hand, unemployment will persist. Third, monetary policy succeeds in defending full employment. However, it cannot overcome long–run instability. Fourth, fiscal policy can circumvent neither unemployment nor long–run instability. And fifth, is monetary policy with continuous budget balance suited to provide both full employment and long–run stability?

In the current section, we shall address monetary policy with continuous budget balance. As a response to a shock, the central bank continuously adjusts the quantity of money so as to ensure full employment at all times. And the government continuously adjusts public consumption so as to always balance the budget. Therefore the short–run equilibrium can be described by a system of seventeen equations:

$$Y = C + I + G + X - Q \tag{1}$$

$$Y = K^{\alpha}N^{\beta} \tag{2}$$

$$K^* = \alpha Y/r \tag{3}$$

$$I = \lambda(K^* - K) \tag{4}$$

$$\dot{K} = I \tag{5}$$

$$T = tY \tag{6}$$

$$G = T \tag{7}$$

$$X = (ep^*/p)^{\theta} \tag{8}$$

$$Q = qC \tag{9}$$

$$\dot{F} = X + (1 - t)rF - Q \tag{10}$$

$$Y + (1 - t)rF = C + S + T \tag{11}$$

$$S = \mu(A^* - A) \tag{12}$$

$$A^* = \beta\delta(1 - t)Y \tag{13}$$

$$A = F + K \tag{14}$$

$$N = \overline{N} \tag{15}$$

$$w/p = \beta Y/N \tag{16}$$

$$M/p = Y/r^{\eta} \tag{17}$$

In this case, α, β, δ, η, θ, λ, μ, p^*, q, r, t, w, F, K and $\overline{N}$ are fixed, whereas e, p, A, A^*, C, $\dot{F}$, G, I, K^*, $\dot{K}$, M, N, Q, S, T, X and Y accommodate themselves.

The short—run equilibrium is isomorphic to that derived for monetary policy in an economy without public sector, cf. (1) until (15) in section 4 of chapter I. As a consequence, the long—run equilibrium will be stable. To summarize, monetary policy with continuous budget balance safeguards both full employment and long—run stability. So far we contemplated flexible monetary policy. Instead we could start from the premise that monetary policy were slow to adapt, cf. section 4.2. in chapter I. In this situation, too, the long—run equilibrium would be stable.

9. TWO COUNTRIES

The research will be carried out within an overlapping generations model. The purpose is to offer a real analysis for flexible wages, cf. sections 1.1. and 5.1. in chapter I. The long–run equilibrium can be represented by a system of seven equations:

$$Y_i = K_i^\alpha \overline{N}_i^\beta \tag{1}$$

$$r = \alpha Y_i / K_i \tag{2}$$

$$G_i + rD_i = t_i(Y_i + rD_i) \tag{3}$$

$$D_1 + D_2 + K_1 + K_2 = \beta\delta(1 - t_1)Y_1 + \beta\delta(1 - t_2)Y_2 \tag{4}$$

Equation (1) states that the countries apply the same technology. By virtue of (2), the interest rate matches the marginal product of capital. What is more, the two interest rates coincide, since capital moves freely. Equation (3) has it that the national budgets are balanced. According to (4), actual wealth agrees with desired wealth. At world level, the foreign assets of country 1 and the foreign debt of country 2 cancel each other. Further imagine that the preference for future consumption δ is uniform across countries. Strictly speaking, α, β, δ, t_i, G_i and $\overline{N}_i$ are exogenous, while r, D_i, K_i and Y_i are endogenous. From (1) and (2) it follows immediately that

$$Y_1/Y_2 = K_1/K_2 = \overline{N}_1/\overline{N}_2 \tag{5}$$

Put another way, labour supply dominates the international allocation of capital and output. On the other hand, tax rates t_i and government purchases G_i have no influence.

For ease of exposition, without losing generality, let labour supply be equal $\overline{N}_1 = \overline{N}_2$. This implies $K_1 = K_2$ and $Y_1 = Y_2$. To simplify matters, disregard the public sector in country 2 $G_2 = t_2 = D_2 = 0$. This does not mean, however, that the countries are just identical. On the contrary, take for instance the goods market equation. Output can be dedicated to private consumption, government purchases and net exports $Y_i = C_i + G_i + H_i$. Admittedly the countries produce the same amount $Y_1 = Y_2$. But they differ in private consumption, government purchases and net exports $C_1 \neq C_2$, $G_1 \neq G_2$, $H_1 = -H_2$. Next have a look at the wealth constraint $A_i = D_i + F_i + K_i$. The countries deviate in private wealth, public debt and foreign assets $A_1 \neq A_2$, $D_1 \neq D_2$, $F_1 = -F_2$. They harmonize merely in the stock of capital $K_1 = K_2$. In addition, because of $t_2 = D_2 = 0$, $K_1 = K_2$ and $Y_1 = Y_2$, (4) can be rewritten as $D_1 + 2K_1 = \beta\delta(2 - t_1)Y_1$.

On these grounds, the long–run equilibrium can be caught by a system of four equations:

$$Y_1 = K_1^\alpha \overline{N}_1^\beta \tag{6}$$
$$r = \alpha Y_1/K_1 \tag{7}$$
$$G_1 + rD_1 = t_1(Y_1 + rD_1) \tag{8}$$
$$D_1 + 2K_1 = \beta\delta(2 - t_1)\,Y_1 \tag{9}$$

Here α, β, δ, t_1, G_1 and $\overline{N}_1$ are given, whereas r, D_1, K_1 and Y_1 adapt themselves.

As a special case, consider the long–run equilibrium without public debt. It serves as a starting point for answering the question how an increase in government purchases impinges on public debt. The long–run equilibrium without public debt can be encapsulated in a system of four equations:

$$Y_1 = K_1^\alpha \overline{N}_1^\beta \tag{10}$$
$$r = \alpha Y_1/K_1 \tag{11}$$
$$G_1 = t_1 Y_1 \tag{12}$$
$$2K_1 = \beta\delta(2 - t_1)Y_1 \tag{13}$$

In this situation, α, β, δ, t_1 and $\overline{N}_1$ are fixed, whereas r, G_1, K_1 and Y_1 accommodate themselves. Above all, government purchases become endogenous.

Now we return to the original system (6) until (9). How does a rise in public consumption bear on output and public debt? In order to solve this problem, express (6) in terms of growth rates $dY_1/Y_1 = \alpha dK_1/K_1$ and $dK_1 = (K_1/\alpha Y_1)dY_1$. Then evaluate this at the long–run equilibrium without public debt (13) to obtain:

$$dK_1 = \frac{\beta\delta(2 - t_1)}{2\alpha} dY_1 \tag{14}$$

After that take the total differential of (9), which yields $dD_1 + 2dK_1 = \beta\delta(2 - t_1)dY_1$. Besides eliminate dK_1 by making use of (14) and rearrange:

$$dD_1 = - \frac{\beta^2\delta(2 - t_1)}{\alpha} dY_1 \tag{15}$$

Similarly take the total differential of (8), which furnishes $dG_1 + (1 - t_1)(D_1 dr + rdD_1) = t_1 dY_1$. Further try to find out its local value at the long–run equilibrium without public debt:

$$dG_1 + (1 - t_1)rdD_1 = t_1 dY_1 \tag{16}$$

Next get rid of r. Locally, at the long–run equilibrium without public debt, it holds $r = 2\alpha/\beta\delta(2 - t_1)$. This can easily be seen by combining (11) and (13). Substitute this into (16) to arrive at:

$$dG_1 + \frac{2\alpha}{\beta\delta} dD_1 = t_1 dY_1 \tag{17}$$

Finally insert (15) into (17) and solve for dY_1:

$$dY_1 = \frac{1}{t_1 + 2\beta(2 - t_1)} dG_1 \tag{18}$$

According to (18), a boost in public consumption elevates output. And by virtue of (15), a lift in output depresses public debt. As a corollary, an increase in public consumption reduces public debt. This seems to be rather paradoxical. Therefore the long–run equilibrium will be unstable. The proof is reminiscent of that given in Carlberg (1992), p. 91.

For the remainder of this section, regard the dynamic effects of a fiscal shock. Initially the economy is in the steady state. In country 1 the budget breaks even, so public debt does not change. In both countries the current account balances, hence foreign assets are uniform. And firms refrain from investment, thus the stock of capital stays put. Moreover let public debt and foreign assets be zero at the start. Against this background, the government in country 1 raises public consumption.

In the short run, this brings the budget of country 1 into deficit. In both countries investment falls. In country 1 net exports drop, while in country 2 they jump up. Country 1 suffers from a current account deficit, but country 2 enjoys a surplus. In country 1 the sum of private and public consumption rises, whereas in country 2 private consumption holds fast. In $Y_1 = C_1 + G_1 + I_1 + H_1$, G_1 goes up and C_1 is constant. I_1 and H_1 decline such that Y_1 remains unaffected. In $Y_2 = C_2 + I_2 + H_2$, correspondingly, I_2 contracts and H_2 expands so as to leave no impact on Y_2 and C_2.

In the medium run, in country 1, the budget deficit leads to the growth of public debt. In both countries, due to the negative investment, the stock of capital withers away. In country 1, the current account deficit contributes to the accumulation of foreign debt. Conversely, in country 2, the current account surplus contributes to the accumulation of foreign assets. What is more, in country 1, the growth of public debt is associated with the growth of public interest, which enlarges the budget deficit, thereby accelerating the growth of public debt. Likewise the accumulation of foreign debt occasions a swelling interest outflow. This in turn worsens the current account deficit and speeds up the accumulation of foreign debt. In country 2, on the other hand, the buildup of foreign assets entails a surging interest inflow, which augments the current account surplus, thus foreign assets build up even faster.

In the long run, in country 1, public debt will tend to explode. In both countries, this drives capital and output down to zero. In country 1, foreign debt proliferates without bounds. In country 2, the other way round, foreign assets grow without limits. In other words, there will be fatal crowding out. Ultimately both economies must break down.

The underlying reason is that country 1 lives beyond its means. Obviously this cannot be sustained. In the real world, there exist three options. First, country 1 tightens its belt. Second, a foreign debt crisis emerges. And third, the world economy collapses, see above. Now the first strategy will be sketched out briefly. In essence, country 1 sharply reduces public consumption so as to transform its budget deficit into a surplus. Therefore public debt begins to decline. In both countries, investment becomes positive, thereby replenishing the stock of capital. In country 1, the current account deficit turns into a surplus, which amortizes foreign debt. Figure 1 stylizes alternative time paths of public consumption. Path 1 is not feasible in the long run, whereas path 2 in fact can be continued.

Instead, a second outcome could be a foreign debt crisis. Due to the heavy load of foreign debt, new credit will no longer be extended. However, the country must repay its old credit. That is why the capital inflow changes into a capital outflow. This induces a severe depreciation that converts the current account surplus into a deficit. As a consequence, the standard of living will be cut back dramatically. In a nutshell, to live beyond one's means is both tempting and dangerous.

Finally some general remarks will be made. The public debt in country 1 displaces private capital in country 1 as well as in country 2. In this sense, the fiscal shock has negative external effects. Half of public debt is foreign debt, so to speak. Compare this to a small open economy. There, as a reaction to an increase in government purchases, public debt tends to blow up. On the other hand, private capital and domestic output remain unaffected. The reason is that, for the small open economy, the world capital market is infinitely large. To conclude, in the closed economy, all of public debt is internal debt. The other way round, in the small open economy, all of public debt is external debt. And in the two—country model, half of public debt is internal debt, the other half being external debt.

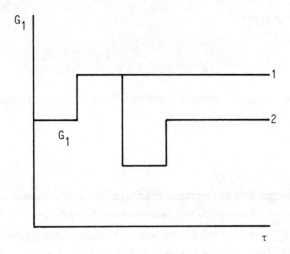

Figure 1
Public Consumption

10. PORTFOLIO MODEL

The wealth of domestic residents consists of three assets, money, government bonds and foreign bonds:

$$A = M + D + eF \tag{1}$$

Here D denotes the stock of government bonds, in terms of domestic currency. And F stands for the stock of foreign bonds, expressed in foreign currency. The quantity of money is given M = const. In the short run, the stocks of government and foreign bonds are fixed, too, D = const, F = const. For the small open economy, the foreign interest rate belongs to the data $r^* =$ const. Government bonds and foreign bonds are perfect substitutes, so the domestic interest rate harmonizes with the foreign interest rate $r = r^*$.

Money demand varies in proportion to wealth $M^d = mA$. In equilibrium, money supply agrees with demand $M = M^d$ or

$$M = mA \tag{2}$$

Similarly, the demand for government and foreign bonds is proportionate to wealth $D^d + eF^d = (1 - m)A$. In equilibrium, the stock meets demand $D + eF = D^d + eF^d$ or

$$D + eF = (1 - m)A \tag{3}$$

The portfolio equilibrium can be characterized by the system of equations (1), (2) and (3). Apparently, one of these equations is redundant. Henceforth, the portfolio equilibrium will be indicated by equations (1) and (2). Here D, F, and M are exogenous, while e and A are endogenous.

Next we shall establish the full short—run equilibrium. Firms produce as much as households, firms, the government and foreigners want to buy $Y = C + I + G + X - Q$. More exactly, Y symbolizes domestic output, C private consumption, I private investment, G public consumption, X exports and Q imports. Without loss of generality, let be $I = 0$. The government imposes a tax and raises loans in order to finance public consumption and the interest payments on public debt. The government acquires a specified volume of goods and services G = const. It pays the interest rate r on public debt D, so public interest amounts to rD. The government collects a tax on both factor income and debt income T = t(Y + rD) with t = const. The excess of public expenditures over tax revenue constitutes the budget deficit G + rD − T. The budget deficit in turn augments public debt $\dot{D}$ = G + rD − T.

At this point, we leave the government budget and enter the current account. Exports are positively correlated with the exchange rate X = e^{θ}, and imports move in proportion to private consumption Q = qC. Domestic residents earn the net interest rate (1 − t)r on foreign assets F, hence the interest inflow totals (1 − t)erF (in domestic currency). The current account surplus is made up of exports and the interest inflow, diminished by imports X + (1 − t)erF − Q. The current account surplus in turn adds to foreign assets $e\dot{F}$ = X + (1 − t)erF − Q (in domestic currency, respectively). By virtue of overlapping generations, cf. section 1, desired wealth is proportionate to domestic income A* = aY. Then private savings are used to overcome the discrepancy between actual and desired wealth round by round S = μ(A* − A), where 0 < μ < 1 is shorthand for the velocity of adaptation. The income of domestic residents embraces domestic income, public interest and the interest inflow. It can be devoted to private consumption, private savings and tax payments Y + rD + (1 − t)erF = C + S + T.

To summarize, the short−run equilibrium can be described by a system of eleven equations:

$$Y = C + G + X - Q \tag{4}$$

$$T = t(Y + rD) \tag{5}$$

$$\dot{D} = G + rD - T \tag{6}$$

$$X = e^{\theta} \tag{7}$$

$$Q = qC \tag{8}$$

$$e\dot{F} = X + (1 - t)erF - Q \tag{9}$$

$$A^* = aY \tag{10}$$

$$A = M + D + eF \tag{11}$$

$$S = \mu(A^* - A) \tag{12}$$

$$Y + rD + (1 - t)erF = C + S + T \tag{13}$$

$$M = mA \tag{14}$$

Here θ, μ, a, m, q, r, t, D, F, G and M are fixed, yet e, A, A^*, C, $\dot{D}$, $\dot{F}$, Q, S, T, X and Y accommodate themselves.

Coming to an end, a few words will be said on the long–run equilibrium. In the steady state, public debt and foreign assets do no longer accumulate $\dot{D} = \dot{F} = 0$. The evaluation of (4) and (13) provides $\dot{D} + e\dot{F} = S$. Owing to $\dot{D} = \dot{F} = 0$, one can infer $S = 0$. Put this into (12) to realize $A^* = A$. Further pay heed to (10) as well as (14) and reshuffle terms $Y = M/am$. Moreover set (6) equal to zero, take account of (5) and solve for D:

$$D = \frac{tY - G}{(1 - t)r} \tag{15}$$

A rise in government purchases lowers public debt, since domestic income does not respond. This appears to be somewhat like a paradox. As a result, the long–run equilibrium will be unstable. This confirms the conclusions drawn in the previous sections.

PART II. FIXED EXCHANGE RATES

It will be assumed here that the central bank stands ready to buy and sell foreign exchange at a fixed rate. In this way, the stock of money becomes endogenous. Apart from this, we shall follow the same avenue as before. To begin with, in chapter I, the basic model will be laid out in greater detail. Then, in chapter II, the public sector will be included in the analysis. The exposition of part II is closely related to that of part I.

Chapter I. Basic Model

1. FLEXIBLE MONEY WAGES

1.1. OVERLAPPING GENERATIONS

In full analogy to part I, the long–run equilibrium can be represented by a system of ten equations:

$$Y = K^{\alpha} \overline{N}^{\beta} \tag{1}$$

$$r = \alpha Y/K \tag{2}$$

$$F + K = \beta \delta Y \tag{3}$$

$$H + rF = 0 \tag{4}$$

$$M/p = Y/r^{\eta} \tag{5}$$

$$w/p = \beta Y/\overline{N} \tag{6}$$

$$Y = C + H \tag{7}$$

$$H = X - Q \tag{8}$$

$$X = (ep^*/p)^{\theta} \tag{9}$$

$$Q = qC \tag{10}$$

In this case α, β, δ, η, θ, e, p^*, q, r and $\overline{N}$ are given, while p, w, C, F, H, K, M, Q, X and Y adjust themselves appropriately. The system (1) until (10) is identical to that obtained for flexible exchange rates, cf. section 1.1. in chapter I of part I. The only difference is that here the exchange rate is exogenous, whereas the quantity of money becomes endogenous.

What are the major attributes of the steady state? All workers have got a job. The current account balances, so foreign assets stay put. Firms abstain from investment, hence domestic capital is uniform. And output does not change, since labour supply is invariant.

Next we shall solve the stationary equilibrium for the endogenous variables. Along the same lines as under flexible exchange rates, one can derive:

$$Y = (\alpha/r)^{\alpha/\beta} \, \overline{N} \tag{11}$$

$$K = (\alpha/r)^{1/\beta} \, \overline{N} \tag{12}$$

$$F = (\beta\delta - \alpha/r)(\alpha/r)^{\alpha/\beta} \, \overline{N} \tag{13}$$

$$H = (\alpha - \beta\delta r)(\alpha/r)^{\alpha/\beta} \, \overline{N} \tag{14}$$

$$C = (\beta + \beta\delta r)(\alpha/r)^{\alpha/\beta} \, \overline{N} \tag{15}$$

$$w/p = \beta(\alpha/r)^{\alpha/\beta} \tag{16}$$

$$R^{\theta} = [1 - (1 - q)(\beta + \beta\delta r)](\alpha/r)^{\alpha/\beta} \, \overline{N} \tag{17}$$

Equations (11) until (17) are isomorphic to those reached for flexible exchange rates. Under flexible exchange rates, it was demonstrated that $e = [1 - (1 - q)(\beta + \beta\delta r)]-r^{\eta}M/p^*$. Under fixed exchange rates, conversely, the stock of money can be stated in terms of the parameters:

$$M = \frac{ep^*}{[1 - (1 - q)(\beta + \beta\delta r)]r^{\eta}} \tag{18}$$

Further eliminate M and Y in (5) with the help of (18) and (11) to gain:

$$p = \frac{(r/\alpha)^{\alpha/\beta}ep^*}{[1 - (1 - q)(\beta + \beta\delta r)]\overline{N}} \tag{19}$$

Evidently this departs from the conclusions drawn for flexible exchange rates. At last substitute (19) into (16) and regroup:

$$w = \frac{\beta ep^*}{[1 - (1 - q)(\beta + \beta\delta r)]\overline{N}} \tag{20}$$

This deviates from flexible exchange rates, too.

How will the economy be affected by macroeconomic shocks? First consider a devaluation of domestic currency. Capital, output, foreign assets, consumption and the trade account do not answer. Merely the quantity of money, money wages and prices are elevated in proportion. The disturbance leaves no impact on real wages and the real exchange rate. Phrased differently, the devaluation has no real effects in the long run. Second suppose that the foreign interest rate jumps up. This disruption depresses capital and output. Locally, foreign assets climb but consumption drops. The trade account deteriorates, yet money wages and prices are inflated. On the other hand, real wages and the real exchange rate come down. This is tantamount to a real appreciation.

Third contemplate an addition to labour supply. This boosts capital, output and consumption proportionately. Locally, foreign assets and the trade account remain untouched. The quantity of money and real wages do not react either. Money wages and prices are pulled down, while the real exchange rate is pushed up, in proportion respectively. This is equivalent to a real depreciation. Fourth imagine that the preference for future consumption rises. This impulse has no influence on capital and output. Foreign assets and consumption improve, whereas the trade account worsens. The stock of money expands, and so do money wages and prices. Real wages stay put, and the real exchange rate declines. For a synopsis, refer to table 3.

Table 3
Long–Run Effects (Flexible Money Wages)

	e ↑	r* ↑	$\overline{N}$ ↑	δ ↑
K	→	↓	↑	→
Y	→	↓	↑	→
F	→	↑	→	↑
C	→	↓	↑	↑
H	→	↓	→	↓
M	↑	?	→	↑
w	↑	↑	↓	↑
p	↑	↑	↓	↑
w/p	→	↓	→	→
ep*/p	→	↓	↑	↓

1.2. SHORT–RUN EQUILIBRIUM, LONG–RUN EQUILIBRIUM
AND STABILITY

The short–run equilibrium can be captured by a system of fifteen equations:

$$Y = C + I + X - Q \tag{1}$$

$$Y = K^{\alpha}N^{\beta} \tag{2}$$

$$K^* = \alpha Y/r \tag{3}$$

$$I = \lambda(K^* - K) \tag{4}$$

$$\dot{K} = I \tag{5}$$

$$X = (ep^*/p)^{\theta} \tag{6}$$

$$Q = qC \tag{7}$$

$$\dot{F} = X + rF - Q \tag{8}$$

$$Y + rF = C + S \tag{9}$$

$$S = \mu(A^* - A) \tag{10}$$

$$A^* = \beta\delta Y \tag{11}$$

$$A = F + K \tag{12}$$

$$N = \overline{N} \tag{13}$$

$$w/p = \beta Y/N \tag{14}$$

$$M/p = Y/r^{\eta} \tag{15}$$

In this case α, β, δ, η, θ, λ, μ, e, p^*, q, r, F, K and $\overline{N}$ are given, whereas p, w, A, A^*, C, $\dot{F}$, I, K^*, $\dot{K}$, M, N, Q, S, X and Y adapt themselves. The system (1) until (15) conforms to that achieved for flexible exchange rates, cf. (1) until (15) in section 1.2. of chapter I part I. The sole distinction is that here the exchange rate is exogenous, while the quantity of money becomes endogenous.

Regard for instance an increase in domestic income which raises money demand. Therefore private agents sell foreign assets to the central bank, thus expanding the quantity of money. Over and above that, the central bank earns interest on the foreign assets just mentioned. We suppose that these earnings are distributed to private agents. In addition, money does not enter the wealth identity. The reason is that including both the stock of foreign assets and the quantity of money would amount to double counting.

The short—run equilibrium can be viewed as a system of two differential equations $\dot{F} = f(F, K)$ and $\dot{K} = g(F, K)$. In the long—run equilibrium, the motion of foreign assets and domestic capital comes to a halt $\dot{F} = \dot{K} = 0$. Beyond that, the long—run equilibrium accords to that found out for overlapping generations, cf. section 1.1. The phase diagram looks like the one drawn for flexible exchange rates, cf. figure 1 in section 1.3. of chapter I part I. As a corollary the long—run equilibrium proves to be stable.

1.3. SHOCKS

In this section, we shall trace out the processes of adjustment released by diverse shocks. For a more detailed analysis, see the export disturbance under fixed money wages in section 2.3. Let us begin with an interest shock. Initially the economy is at rest in the long—run equilibrium. Particularly the labour market clears. The current account balances, so foreign assets do not build up. Firms do without investment, hence domestic capital is uniform. Besides let domestic residents hold no foreign assets at the start. Under these circumstances, the foreign interest rate rises. In the phase diagram, the $\dot{F} = 0$ line shifts to the right, and the $\dot{K} = 0$ line travels downwards, cf. figure 1.

In the short run, capital flows out, thereby enhancing the domestic interest rate. This impedes investment and output, thus unemployment comes into existence. Instantaneously, as a response, money wages drop, which compels firms to reduce prices. That is why exports and output spring up, in this way restoring full employment.

In the medium run, by virtue of the current account surplus, foreign assets pile up round by round. And the negative investment dismantles the stock of capital. Further the decline in capital goes along with a decline in output. Moreover the decline in capital raises marginal cost and prices, which lowers exports and the current account surplus. And investment recovers as the stock of capital dwindles.

Over time the economy gravitates to a new long—run equilibrium. Still all workers have got a job. The current account balances again, so foreign assets do no longer accumulate. And firms stop to disinvest, hence the stock of capital does not wither away any more. Strictly speaking, a substantial amount of foreign assets has been heaped up during transition. On the other hand, the terminal stock of capital falls short of the initial one. Similarly output has settled down at a deeper level.

Second consider a labour supply shock. Originally the economy is in the steady state. In this situation, labour supply increases spontaneously. In the phase diagram, the $\dot{F} = 0$ line is transferred to the right, whereas the $\dot{K} = 0$ line moves upwards, cf. figure 2 in section 1.4. of chapter I part I. In the short term, due to the emerging

134

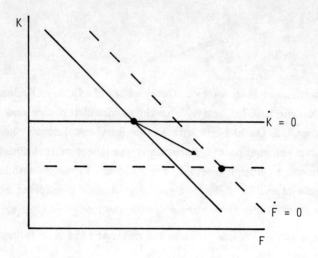

Figure 1
Interest Shock

unemployment, money wages and prices are cut back immediately, which stimulates exports and output. The addition to income causes an addition to investment. And firms engage more workers as output rises, thereby bringing back full employment.

In the intermediate term, owing to the current account surplus, foreign assets accumulate. And the positive investment makes the stock of capital grow. Beyond that, the expansion of capital is associated with an expansion of output. Wealth mounts, and so do consumption as well as imports. Hence, after some time, the surplus on current account turns into a deficit. And investment recedes to the extent that the stock of capital has been adjusted. Eventually the economy converges to a new steady state. In the end, foreign assets again disappear from the scene, while the stock of capital is larger than before.

Third imagine a savings shock. At the beginning, the economy is in the stationary equilibrium. Against this background, the preference for future consumption climbs on its own. In the phase diagram, the $\dot{F} = 0$ line glides to the right, cf. figure 3 in section 1.4. of chapter I part I. In the short run, savings improve but consumption and output deteriorate. On behalf of the accompanying unemployment, money wages and prices are curtailed. This advances exports and output, thus reinstating full employment. In the medium run, the current account surplus contributes to the building up of foreign assets. This boosts wealth, consumption and imports, so the current account surplus shrinks. As time proceeds, the economy reaches a new stationary equilibrium. A specified volume of foreign assets has been heaped up during transition, yet domestic capital did not stir.

Fourth an exchange rate shock will be treated. At the start, let the economy be in the permanent equilibrium. Then, suddenly, domestic currency is revalued. In the short run, exports and output decline, hence unemployment occurs. For that reason, money wages and prices drop. This encourages exports and output, thereby curing unemployment. To conclude, the disturbance has no real effects, neither transitorily nor permanently. In the phase diagram nothing happens. Fifth a few words will be said on an export shock. Initially the economy is in the long–run equilibrium. Under these circumstances, exports plunge. In the short run, prices plummet too, thus putting back exports. To summarize, the disruption does not impinge on the real sector, neither in the short run nor in the long run. Sixth catch a glimpse of a foreign price shock. Originally the economy is in the steady state. Then, abruptly, the price of foreign goods descends. In the short term, this lowers exports. As a reaction, the price of domestic goods is marked down as well, which reestablishes exports. Accordingly, the impulse has no real consequences whatsoever.

Seventh contemplate an investment shock. At the beginning, the economy is at rest in the stationary equilibrium. In this situation, investment worsens autonomously. For the streamline refer to figure 3 in section 1.4. of chapter I part I. In the short run, the disturbance pulls down prices and pushes up exports, so output remains unaffected. The negative investment dismantles the stock of capital, and the current account surplus piles up foreign assets. In the medium run, investment recovers endogenously. This in turn elevates prices and depresses exports. By virtue of the positive investment, the stock of capital becomes refilled period by period. And because of the current account deficit, foreign assets are being given back. At last the post–shock steady state coincides with the pre–shock steady state.

2. FIXED MONEY WAGES

2.1. OVERLAPPING GENERATIONS

In the current section, we postulate fixed money wages. With this exception, we take the same approach as before. As a frame of reference, consider the long–run equilibrium for flexible money wages, cf. (1) until (10) in section 1.1. The only difference is that here $Y = K^\alpha N^\beta$ and $w/p = \beta Y/N$ are substituted for (1) and (6), respectively. On that grounds, the long–run equilibrium can be laid out as follows:

$$Y = K^\alpha N^\beta \tag{1}$$

$$r = \alpha Y/K \tag{2}$$

$$F + K = \beta \delta Y \tag{3}$$

$$H + rF = 0 \tag{4}$$

$$M/p = Y/r^\eta \tag{5}$$

$$w/p = \beta Y/N \tag{6}$$

$$Y = C + H \tag{7}$$

$$H = X - Q \tag{8}$$

$$X = (ep^*/p)^\theta \tag{9}$$

$$Q = qC \tag{10}$$

In this case α, β, δ, η, θ, e, p^*, q, r and w are given, whereas p, C, F, H, K, M, N, Q, X and Y adapt themselves. Money wages are exogenous, while labour demand becomes endogenous, as opposed to flexible money wages. Generally the economy will suffer from underemployment (or overemployment).

What are the principal characteristics of the steady state? The labour market does not clear, as has just been mentioned. The current account breaks even, so foreign assets remain unchanged. Firms do without investment, hence the stock of capital is uniform. Both labour demand and output are constant.

At this juncture, the endogenous variables will be stated explicitly. In full analogy to flexible money wages, one obtains:

$$Y = (\alpha/r)^{\alpha/\beta}N \tag{11}$$

$$K = (\alpha/r)^{1/\beta}N \tag{12}$$

$$F = (\beta\delta - \alpha/r)(\alpha/r)^{\alpha/\beta}N \tag{13}$$

$$H = (\alpha - \beta\delta r)(\alpha/r)^{\alpha/\beta}N \tag{14}$$

$$C = (\beta + \beta\delta r)(\alpha/r)^{\alpha/\beta}N \tag{15}$$

$$w/p = \beta(\alpha/r)^{\alpha/\beta} \tag{16}$$

$$M = \frac{ep^*}{[1 - (1 - q)(\beta + \beta\delta r)]r^{\eta}} \tag{17}$$

There is one small departure, however, namely that labour demand becomes endogenous. Now combine (5) and (6) to arrive at $N = \beta r^{\eta}M/w$. Then get rid of M with the help of (17) and rearrange:

$$N = \frac{\beta ep^*}{[1 - (1 - q)(\beta + \beta\delta r)]w} \tag{18}$$

Clearly this deviates from the results found for flexible money wages.

How do macroeconomic shocks bear on the steady state? First suppose that domestic currency is devalued. This raises capital, labour demand, output, consumption and the quantity of money in proportion. Locally, foreign assets and the trade account do not answer. Prices and real wages are invariant, merely the real exchange rate goes up. That is to say, the disturbance has real effects, in contrast to flexible money wages. Second, a rise in the foreign interest rate supports employment and inflates prices. On the other hand, real wages and the real exchange rate fall. Third, an increase in the preference for future consumption boosts capital, labour demand, output, consumption and the quantity of money. Locally, foreign assets and the trade account stay put. Likewise prices, real wages, and the real exchange rate hold fast. Fourth, a lift in money wages depresses capital, labour demand, output and consumption in proportion. Conversely, it enhances prices in proportion. Locally, foreign assets and the trade account remain untouched. The disruption leaves no impact on the quantity of money and real wages, but lowers the real exchange rate. Table 4 presents an overview of these findings.

Table 4
Long—Run Effects (Fixed Money Wages)

	e ↑	r* ↑	δ ↑	w ↑
K	↑	?	↑	↓
N	↑	↑	↑	↓
Y	↑	?	↑	↓
F	→	?	→	→
C	↑	?	↑	↓
H	→	?	→	→
M	↑	?	↑	→
p	→	↑	→	↑
w/p	→	↓	→	→
ep*/p	↑	↓	→	↓

2.2. SHORT–RUN EQUILIBRIUM, LONG–RUN EQUILIBRIUM
AND STABILITY

As a baseline, contemplate the short–run equilibrium for flexible money wages, cf. (1) until (15) in section 1.2. The sole divergence is that here money wages are exogenous, while labour demand becomes endogenous. For that reason, $N = \overline{N}$ does no longer apply. As a rule, there will be underemployment (or overemployment). The short–run equilibrium can be interpreted as a system of two differential equations $\dot{F} = f(F, K)$ and $\dot{K} = g(F, K)$. In the long–run equilibrium, the motion of foreign assets and domestic capital comes to a standstill $\dot{F} = \dot{K} = 0$. As a consequence, the long–run equilibrium will be identical to that deduced for overlapping generations, cf. (1) until (10) in section 2.1. For the properties see above.

In doing the stability analysis, to simplify matters, we posit $I = 0$. Accordingly, the short–run equilibrium can be described by a system of eleven equations:

$$Y = C + X - Q \tag{1}$$

$$Y = K^{\alpha}N^{\beta} \tag{2}$$

$$X = (ep^*/p)^{\theta} \tag{3}$$

$$Q = qC \tag{4}$$

$$\dot{F} = X + rF - Q \tag{5}$$

$$Y + rF = C + S \tag{6}$$

$$S = \mu(A^* - A) \tag{7}$$

$$A^* = \beta\delta Y \tag{8}$$

$$A = F + K \tag{9}$$

$$w/p = \beta Y/N \tag{10}$$

$$M/p = Y/r^{\eta} \tag{11}$$

In this case α, β, δ, η, θ, μ, e, p^*, q, r, w, F and $\dot{K}$ are fixed, whereas p, A, A^*, C, $\dot{F}$, M, N, Q, S, X and Y accommodate themselves.

Next a few remarks will be made on the attributes of the short–run equilibrium. Insert (8) and (9) into (7) to accomplish the savings function:

$$S = \beta\delta\mu Y - \mu(F + K) \tag{12}$$

Then eliminate S in (5) by means of (12) to gain the consumption function:

$$C = (1 - \beta\delta\mu)Y + rF + \mu(F + K) \tag{13}$$

Further, letting be $\theta = e = p^* = 1$, (3) assumes the shape $X = 1/p$. Amalgamate (2) and (10), which yields $p = (w/\beta)(Y/K)^{\alpha/\beta}$. Moreover put this into $X = 1/p$:

$$X = (\beta/w)(K/Y)^{\alpha/\beta} \tag{14}$$

Last but not least, join (1) with (4), (13) as well as (14) and solve for:

$$(1 - q)(\mu + r)F = [1 - (1 - q)(1 - \beta\delta\mu)]Y - (\beta/w)(K/Y)^{\alpha/\beta} - (1 - q)\mu K \tag{15}$$

Obviously the short–run equilibrium can be compressed to a single differential equation $\dot{F} = f(F)$. In the long–run equilibrium, foreign assets cease to move $\dot{F} = 0$. Here the stock of capital becomes exogenous, contrary to overlapping generations. That is why $r = \alpha Y/K$ is no longer valid. On the one hand, (18) in section 2.1. still applies. On the other hand,

$$Y = K^{\alpha}\{\beta ep^*/[1 - (1 - q)(\beta + \beta\delta r)]w\}^{\beta} \tag{16}$$

takes the place of (11) in section 2.1. This can be demonstrated by merging $Y = K^{\alpha}N^{\beta}$ and (18) from section 2.1.

The confrontation of (1) and (6) delivers $S = X + rF - Q$ and, together with (5), $\dot{F} = S$. Now observe (12) to reach $\dot{F} = \beta\delta\mu Y - \mu(F + K)$, then differentiate for F:

$$d\dot{F}/dF = \beta\delta\mu dY/dF - \mu \tag{17}$$

To get rid of dY/dF, differentiate (15) for Y and evaluate the derivative at the long–run equilibrium with (16). After some manipulations, this leads to a critical level of the interest rate:

$$r' = \frac{\alpha + \beta q - \alpha\beta(1 - q)}{\beta\delta(1 - q)} \tag{18}$$

If $r \lessgtr r'$ then $d\dot{F}/dF \lessgtr 0$. In other words, when the foreign interest rate is low, the long–run equilibrium will be stable. The other way round, when the foreign interest rate is high, the long–run equilibrium will be unstable. This resembles the outcome for flexible exchange rates and flexible money wages, provided there are capital gains. For the case $I = 0$, the critical level was $r' = [q + \alpha(1 - q)]/\beta\delta(1 - q)$.

2.3. EXPORT SHOCK

At the beginning, the economy is in the steady state. The current account balances, so foreign assets do not alter. At the start, let domestic residents hold no foreign assets, and let all workers get a job. In this situation, exports decline autonomously. In the short term, this reduces output, hence firms have to dismiss workers. The disturbance has real consequences, as opposed to the case of flexible money wages.

In the intermediate term, due to the current account deficit, foreign debt accumulates. The diminution in wealth goes along with a diminution in consumption and output, thereby increasing unemployment. With respect to current account dynamics, there are two channels of transmission. First the fall in wealth contracts consumption and imports, which lowers the current account deficit. Second the growth of foreign debt expands the interest outflow, thus raising the current account deficit. What is the net effect? If the foreign interest rate is small, the interest outflow will be small, too. Therefore the current account deficit shrinks, so the steady state will be stable. Conversely, if the foreign interest rate is large, the interest outflow will be large as well. Because of that the current account deficit swells, hence the steady state will be unstable.

Now suppose that the foreign interest rate is low. Under these circumstances, the current account deficit diminishes wealth and imports, thereby mitigating the current account deficit. The steady state will be stable. In the long–term equilibrium, unemployment still persists. The current account balances again, so foreign assets do not change any more. Strictly speaking, a certain volume of foreign debt has been piled up during transition. The time path of output is illustrated in figure 1, and the trajectory of labour demand looks very similar.

Instead imagine that the foreign interest rate is high. In this case, the current account deficit augments foreign debt and the interest outflow, thus exacerbating the current account deficit. The steady state will be unstable. In the long term, foreign debt tends to explode, which squeezes wealth down to zero. The same applies to consumption, output and labour demand. In the end, the economy must collapse. Over and above that, assume that investment and capital are permitted to adjust freely. Under these conditions, the decline in income is accompanied by a decline in investment, hence the stock of capital becomes dismantled. Figure 2 portrays the

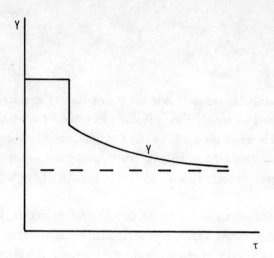

Figure 1
Fixed Money Wages (Stable Case)

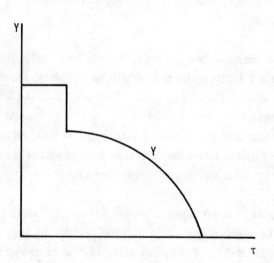

Figure 2
Fixed Money Wages (Unstable Case)

time path of output for the unstable branch. The associated trajectory of labour demand can be drawn in the same way.

In summary, the economy enters a vicious circle of current account deficit, foreign debt and interest outflow. There domestic residents borrow abroad in order to finance the interest payments on foreign debt. This holds in contradistinction to flexible money wages, where the long–term equilibrium proved to be stable. From this point of view, fixed money wages are a potential factor of instability. Likewise, under flexible exchange rates, the long–term equilibrium turned out to be stable. Correspondingly, fixed exchange rates are a potential factor of instability, too. In this sense, flexible exchange rates are superior to fixed exchange rates.

3. SLOW MONEY WAGES

In the current section, we add wage dynamics. The rate of change of money wages is a decreasing function of the rate of unemployment $\dot{w} = \epsilon w(N/\overline{N} - 1)$. Apart from this, we follow the same lines as before. For ease of exposition, let be $I = 0$. The short–run equilibrium can be captured by a system of twelve equations:

$$Y = C + X - Q \tag{1}$$

$$Y = K^{\alpha}N^{\beta} \tag{2}$$

$$X = (ep^*/p)^{\theta} \tag{3}$$

$$Q = qC \tag{4}$$

$$\dot{F} = X + rF - Q \tag{5}$$

$$Y + rF = C + S \tag{6}$$

$$S = \mu(A^* - A) \tag{7}$$

$$A^* = \beta\delta Y \tag{8}$$

$$A = F + K \tag{9}$$

$$\dot{w} = \epsilon w(N/\overline{N} - 1) \tag{10}$$

$$w/p = \beta Y/N \tag{11}$$

$$M/p = Y/r^{\eta} \tag{12}$$

Here α, β, δ, η, θ, μ, e, p^*, q, r, w, F, K and $\overline{N}$ are exogenous, while p, $\dot{w}$, A, A^*, C, $\dot{F}$, M, N, Q, S, X and Y are endogenous.

The short–run equilibrium can be condensed to a system of two differential equations $\dot{w} = f(w, F)$ and $\dot{F} = g(w, F)$. In the long–run equilibrium, the motion of money wages and foreign assets comes to a halt. Besides, the long–run equilibrium under slow money wages agrees with the long–run equilibrium under flexible money wages. Under flexible money wages, the long–run equilibrium is stable. Under fixed money wages, on the other hand, stability is subject to a condition. Therefore one may expect that under slow money wages there will be a condition as well.

For the remainder of this section, we shall keep track of the process of adjustment induced by an export shock. In this connection it is helpful to distinguish between the stable and the unstable case. Let us begin with the stable branch. Initially the economy is in the stationary equilibrium. The labour market clears. The current account breaks even, so foreign assets are invariant. At the start, let there be no foreign assets at all. Then, abruptly, exports come down. In the short run, this curbs output, thereby giving rise to unemployment. In the medium run, money wages and prices begin to deflate. This stimulates exports and output, thus alleviating unemployment. Eventually the economy reaches a new stationary equilibrium. Full employment will be regained. Once more the current account breaks even, and foreign debt has evaporated. In other words, the export shock has real effects in the short run. However, is has no real consequences in the long run. Figure 1 visualizes the pertinent time path of output.

Next we deal with the unstable branch. Originally the economy is in the steady state. In this situation, again, exports deteriorate. In the short term, this depresses output, so firms have to lay off workers. In the intermediate term, owing to the current account deficit, foreign debt builds up. Concomitantly, the interest outflow surges, thus enlarging the current account deficit. Wealth contracts, and so do consumption as well as output, which reinforces unemployment. In the long term, foreign debt grows without limits, thereby driving output down to zero. Figure 2 reveals the trajectory of output.

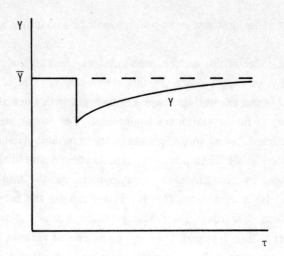

Figure 1
Slow Money Wages (Stable Case)

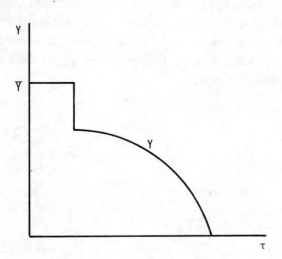

Figure 2
Slow Money Wages (Unstable Case)

4. PORTFOLIO MODEL

The investigation will be carried out within a simple framework. For the small open economy, the foreign interest rate is given $r^* = $ const. Domestic and foreign bonds are perfect substitutes, so the domestic interest rate accords with the foreign interest rate $r = r^*$. The portfolio equilibrium can be encapsulated in a system of two equations:

$$A = M + B + eF \tag{1}$$

$$M = mA \tag{2}$$

By virtue of (1), the wealth of domestic residents consists of domestic money, domestic bonds and foreign bonds. Equation (2) states that money supply satisfies money demand. Here e, A and B are exogenous, whereas F and M are endogenous. Compare this with a regime of flexible exchange rates. There B, F and M are fixed, while e and A accommodate themselves.

Now consider an increase in wealth, say due to a current account surplus. Take the total differential of (1) and (2) to verify $dM = mdA$ and $edF = (1 - m)dA$. Owing to that, the increase in wealth raises the stocks of both domestic money and foreign bonds. The underlying mechanism is that private agents receive foreign exchange equal in amount to the current account surplus, which enlarges their wealth. As a response, they convert part of the foreign exchange into domestic money and part into foreign bonds.

Next the full short–run equilibrium will be installed. Consumption, exports and imports determine domestic output $Y = C + X - Q$. For the sake of convenience, investment will be disregarded. Exports are autonomous $X = \overline{X}$, and imports vary in proportion to domestic income $Q = qY$. The income of domestic residents can be devoted to consumption and savings $Y + rF = C + S$. The savings function is $S = \mu(A^* - A)$, where desired wealth is proportionate to domestic income $A^* = aY$. Of course, savings contribute to the accumulation of wealth $\dot{A} = S$.

Therefore the short–run equilibrium can be represented by a system of nine equations:

$$Y = C + X - Q \tag{3}$$

$$X = \overline{X} \tag{4}$$

$$Q = qY \tag{5}$$

$$Y + rF = C + S \tag{6}$$

$$S = \mu(A^* - A) \tag{7}$$

$$A^* = aY \tag{8}$$

$$A = M + B + F \tag{9}$$

$$M = mA \tag{10}$$

$$\dot{A} = S \tag{11}$$

In this case μ, a, m, q, r, A, B and $\overline{X}$ are constant, but $\dot{A}$, A^*, C, F, M, Q, S, X and Y are variable.

At this juncture, we shall ascertain the long–run equilibrium. The short–run equilibrium can be viewed as a single differential equation $\dot{A} = f(A)$. In the long–run equilibrium, wealth stops to adjust $\dot{A} = 0$. Substitute this into (11) to get S = 0. Further insert S = 0 into (6) and solve for C = Y + rF. In addition we shall elimina- te F. For this purpose, combine S = 0 and (7), which yields A = A^*. Note (8) and (9) to find out M + B + F = aY. From (10) and A = aY it follows that M = amY. Put this into M + B + F = aY and regroup F = (1 − m)aY − B. Then get rid of F in C = Y + rF, which furnishes:

$$C = Y + (1 - m)arY - rB \tag{12}$$

Finally place (4), (5) and (12) into the right–hand side of (3) and reshuffle terms:

$$Y = \frac{\overline{X} - (1 - q)rB}{q - (1 - m)(1 - q)ar} \tag{13}$$

Here the question arises how output is affected by a spontaneous increase in exports. Correspondingly, the evaluation of (13) leads to a critical level of the interest rate:

$$r' = \frac{q}{a(1 - m)(1 - q)} \tag{14}$$

As long as the foreign interest rate stays below the critical level, the increase in exports pushes up output. However, as soon as the foreign interest rate surpasses the critical level, the increase in exports pulls down output. This seems to be somewhat like a paradox. For that reason one may suspect that in this case the steady state will be unstable. This result is structurally identical to that obtained in section 2, for an elaborate stability analysis see there.

To illustrate this, have a look at an export shock. Originally the economy is in the steady state. In particular the current account breaks even. At the start, let all workers get a job, and let domestic residents hold foreign assets. Against this background, exports decline spontaneously. In the short term, this puts a brake on output, so unemployment looms. In the intermediate term, owing to the current account deficit, wealth comes down period by period. This in turn cuts back the holdings of both foreign assets and domestic money. In addition, the fall in wealth entails a fall in consumption and output. As far as the current account is concerned, two opposing forces are at work. On the one hand, the diminution in imports alleviates the current account deficit. On the other hand, the shrinking of the interest inflow aggravates the current account deficit. What is the net effect? If the foreign interest rate is small, the current account deficit dwindles, hence the steady state will be stable. Conversely, if the foreign interest rate is large, the current account deficit surges, thus the steady state will be unstable. Naturally the time paths are equivalent to those constructed in section 2.3.

Chapter II. Economy with Public Sector

Now the public sector will be incorporated into the analysis. The government levies an income tax and raises loans in order to finance government purchases and the interest payments on public debt. The budget deficit in turn augments public debt. The research will be implemented within an IS–LM model featuring the dynamics of public debt, foreign assets, private capital and money wages.

1. FLEXIBLE MONEY WAGES

To simplify matters, we posit $I = 0$ and $K = $ const. In this case, the short–run equilibrium can be summed up by a system of fourteen equations:

$$Y = C + G + X - Q \tag{1}$$

$$Y = K^{\alpha}N^{\beta} \tag{2}$$

$$T = t(Y + rD) \tag{3}$$

$$\dot{D} = G + rD - T \tag{4}$$

$$X = (ep^*/p)^{\theta} \tag{5}$$

$$Q = qC \tag{6}$$

$$\dot{F} = X + (1 - t)rF - Q \tag{7}$$

$$Y + rD + (1 - t)rF = C + S + T \tag{8}$$

$$S = \mu(A^* - A) \tag{9}$$

$$A^* = \beta\delta(1 - t)Y \tag{10}$$

$$A = D + F + K \tag{11}$$

$$N = \overline{N} \tag{12}$$

$$w/p = \beta Y/N \tag{13}$$

$$M/p = Y/r^{\eta} \tag{14}$$

Here p, w, A, A^*, C, $\dot{D}$, $\dot{F}$, M, N, Q, S, T, X and Y adjust themselves. As an implication, the short–run equilibrium harmonizes with that reached for flexible exchange rates, cf. (1) until (14) in section 2.2. of chapter I part I. The only difference is that in this instance e is exogenous, while M becomes endogenous.

The short–run equilibrium can be compressed to a system of two differential equations $\dot{D} = f(D, F)$ and $\dot{F} = g(D, F)$. In the long–run equilibrium, public debt and foreign assets cease to move. The phase diagram is isomorphic to that derived for flexible exchange rates. As a fundamental implication, the long–run equilibrium proves to be unstable. This is in clear contradistinction to the basic model where the long–run equilibrium turned out to be stable. Phrased differently, the introduction of the public sector creates long–run instability.

Consider for example the dynamics of a fiscal shock. At the beginning, the economy is at rest in the long–run equilibrium. Of course the labour market clears. Both the budget and the current account balance, so public debt and foreign assets are uniform. What is more, let public debt and foreign assets be zero at the start. Under these circumstances, the government raises its purchases of goods and services. In the short run, this enhances output, hence overemployment arises. Instantaneously, as a response, money wages and prices spring up, which impedes exports and output, thereby restoring full employment. The addition to government purchases brings the budget into deficit. Similarly, the reduction of exports moves the current account into deficit. Properly speaking, the current account deficit coincides with the budget deficit. In this sense, indirectly, the government borrows abroad.

In the medium run, by virtue of the budget deficit, public debt accumulates round by round. And because of the current account deficit, foreign debt builds up. More precisely, foreign debt is the same size as public debt. Therefore private wealth, private consumption and output remain unchanged. The growth of public debt entails a swell of public interest. This in turn augments the budget deficit, thus speeding up the growth of public debt. Likewise the expansion of foreign debt is accompanied by a surging interest outflow, which enlarges the current account deficit, in this way reinforcing the expansion of foreign debt. In the long run, public and foreign debt are bound to explode. In summary, the economy enters a vicious circle, where the government borrows at home in order to finance the interest payments on public debt. As a consequence, domestic residents borrow abroad in order to finance the interest payments on foreign debt.

Now what problems are involved in long–run instability? In the model, no problem does exist. Output, private consumption and private wealth are stable, merely public and foreign debt are unstable. The underlying reason is that budget deficits are financed by raising loans abroad. In the small open economy, the foreign interest rate does not react. That is why there will be no displacement of private investment. But in the real world, as public and foreign debt proliferate without bounds, the economy is no longer small. Instead, this drives up the foreign interest rate, thus dampening private investment. Both capital and output drop. As the foreign interest rate grows without limits, capital and output shrink back to zero.

Obviously this is not efficient. In due course, the government must lift the tax rate. The later this happens, the larger the lift must be. A straightforward solution would be to equilibrate the budget at all times, cf. section 4.

2. FIXED MONEY WAGES

As a baseline, take the short–run equilibrium under flexible money wages, cf. (1) until (14) in section 1. The sole departure is that here money wages are exogenous, while labour demand becomes endogenous. $N = \overline{N}$ does not hold any more, instead the economy suffers from underemployment (or overemployment). For the sake of convenience, let firms do without investment $I = 0$.

Accordingly, the short–run equilibrium can be caught by a system of thirteen equations:

$$Y = C + G + X - Q \tag{1}$$

$$Y = K^{\alpha}N^{\beta} \tag{2}$$

$$T = t(Y + rD) \tag{3}$$

$$\dot{D} = G + rD - T \tag{4}$$

$$X = (ep^*/p)^{\theta} \tag{5}$$

$$Q = qC \tag{6}$$

$$\dot{F} = X + (1-t)rF - Q \tag{7}$$

$$Y + rD + (1-t)rF = C + S + T \tag{8}$$

$$S = \mu(A^* - A) \tag{9}$$

$$A^* = \beta\delta(1-t)Y \tag{10}$$

$$A = D + F + K \tag{11}$$

$$w/p = \beta Y/N \tag{12}$$

$$M/p = Y/r^{\eta} \tag{13}$$

In this case p, A, A^*, C, $\dot{D}$, $\dot{F}$, M, N, Q, S, T, X and Y adapt themselves suitably.

The short–run equilibrium can be condensed to a system of two differential equations $\dot{D} = f(D, F)$ and $\dot{F} = g(D, F)$. In the long–run equilibrium, public debt and foreign assets stop to adjust. As a principal result, the long–run equilibrium turns out to be unstable. The proof resembles that given for flexible money wages. Compare this to the basic model, where long–run stability was subject to a condition. In other words, the presence of the public sector creates long–run instability.

To throw some light on this point, regard for instance an export shock. Initially the economy is in the stationary equilibrium. The budget and the current account break even. At the start, let all workers get a job, and let domestic residents hold neither government nor foreign bonds. In this situation, exports come down. In the short term, the disturbance depresses output, giving rise to unemployment. The cut in exports brings the current account into deficit. The decline in income causes a decline in tax proceeds, so the budget moves into deficit. Further, the fall in income goes along with a fall in private savings.

In the intermediate term, owing to the budget deficit, public debt begins to accumulate. In full analogy, due to the current account deficit, foreign debt accumulates. And by virtue of the negative savings, private wealth decumulates. The drop of private wealth is associated with a drop of private consumption and output, which exacerbates unemployment. Over and above that, as public debt grows, the government has to pay more interest. This amplifies the budget deficit, thereby accelerating the growth of public debt. Likewise, as foreign debt grows, domestic residents have to pay more interest. This boosts the current account deficit, thus foreign debt grows even faster. Finally public and foreign debt tend to blow up.

But in the real world, as foreign debt proliferates without bounds, the foreign interest rate jumps up. In the short term, less capital flows in, hence the domestic interest rate mounts, too. This hampers private investment, aggregate demand and output, so firms have to lay off more workers. In the intermediate term, on account of the negative investment, the stock of capital withers away. Beyond that, this reduces output from the supply side. Ultimately, as foreign debt grows without limits, the foreign interest rate becomes extremely large. This in turn squeezes capital and output down to zero.

3. SLOW MONEY WAGES

The rate of change of money wages is a decreasing function of the rate of unemployment. As compared to flexible money wages, $\dot{w} = \epsilon w(N/\overline{N} - 1)$ is substituted for (12). Apart from this, we take the same approach as before. The short—run equilibrium can be interpreted as a system of three differential equations $\dot{w} = f(w, D, F)$, $\dot{D} = g(w, D, F)$ and $\dot{F} = h(w, D, F)$. In the long—run equilibrium, the movement of money wages, public debt and foreign assets comes to a standstill. The long—run equilibrium under slow money wages agrees with the long—run equilibrium under flexible money wages. As a major consequence, the long—run equilibrium under slow money wages proves to be unstable. This underlines the importance of the conclusions drawn for flexible and fixed money wages.

4. CONTINUOUS BUDGET BALANCE

In the preceding sections, as a rule, we assumed that the government sets public consumption and the tax rate independently. In the current section, as an exception, we suppose continuous budget balance. As a response to a shock, the government continuously adjusts public consumption so as to always balance the budget. On that grounds, public debt does not come into existence. In this context, we posit slow money wages and exclude private investment.

The short–run equilibrium conforms with that obtained for flexible exchange rates, cf. (1) until (14) in section 5 of chapter II part I. The sole deviation is that here the exchange rate is exogenous, while the quantity of money becomes endogenous. What is more, the system is structurally identical to the one established for an economy without public sector, cf. (1) until (12) in section 3 of chapter I part II. As a corollary, there will be a condition for long–run stability.

To illuminate this, consider an export shock, focusing on the stable case. Suddenly exports decline. In the short run, the disturbance pulls down output. As tax earnings diminish, the government has to cut its spending on goods and services. This in turn aggravates the downswing of output. In the medium run, output recovers on its own. As more taxes are paid, the government must buy more goods and services, thereby pushing up output even more. In real terms, the post–shock steady state is equivalent to the pre–shock steady state.

Confront this with an economy where budget deficits are allowed to occur. There the long–run equilibrium proved to be unstable. To sum up, continuous budget balance can restore long–run stability. On the other hand, it increases the fluctuations of income and employment. The other way round, public debt is a factor of long–run instability.

5. FISCAL POLICY

Now we postulate flexible fiscal policy. As a response to a shock, the government continuously adjusts public consumption so as to maintain full employment at all times. Correspondingly, there is no reason why money wages should move. Can this strategy be sustained? To simplify matters, we neglect private investment.

The short—run equilibrium can be written as a system of fourteen equations:

$$Y = C + G + X - Q \tag{1}$$

$$Y = K^{\alpha}N^{\beta} \tag{2}$$

$$T = t(Y + rD) \tag{3}$$

$$\dot{D} = G + rD - T \tag{4}$$

$$X = (ep^*/p)^{\theta} \tag{5}$$

$$Q = qC \tag{6}$$

$$\dot{F} = X + (1-t)rF - Q \tag{7}$$

$$Y + rD + (1-t)rF = C + S + T \tag{8}$$

$$S = \mu(A^* - A) \tag{9}$$

$$A^* = \beta\delta(1-t)Y \tag{10}$$

$$A = D + F + K \tag{11}$$

$$N = \overline{N} \tag{12}$$

$$w/p = \beta Y/N \tag{13}$$

$$M/p = Y/r^{\eta} \tag{14}$$

In this case p, A, A^*, C, $\dot{D}$, $\dot{F}$, G, M, N, Q, S, T, X and Y accommodate themselves. The short—run equilibrium harmonizes with that derived for flexible money wages, cf. (1) until (14) in section 1. The only distinction is that here public consumption is endogenous, while money wages are exogenous.

Next we shall discuss the stability of the long–run equilibrium. By virtue of $Y = K^{\alpha}\,\overline{N}^{\beta}$, output is constant since capital and labour supply are invariant. Further solve (12) and (13) for p and insert the resulting term into (5), which delivers $X = (\beta ep^*Y/w\overline{N})^{\theta}$. The right–hand side is uniform, which can be noted as $X = \overline{X}$. Besides reformulate (8):

$$C \;=\; Y + rD + (1-t)rF - S - T \tag{15}$$

Then eliminate C, X and Q in (1) by making use of (15), $X = \overline{X}$ and (6) to reach fiscal policy:

$$G \;=\; qY - (1-q)[rD + (1-t)rF - S - T] - \overline{X} \tag{16}$$

Beyond that put (16) into (4), paying attention to the savings function $S = \beta\delta\mu(1 - t)Y - \mu(D + F + K)$ and (3):

$$
\begin{aligned}
\dot{D} \;=\;\; & (1-t)qY + (1-q)(1-t)\beta\delta\mu Y + (1-t)qrD - (1-q)\mu D \\
& - (1-q)[\mu + (1-t)r]F - (1-q)\mu K - \overline{X}
\end{aligned}
\tag{17}
$$

In addition differentiate (17) for D, which gives rise to a critical level of the interest rate. If $r \lessgtr (1-q)\mu/(1-t)q$, then $\partial\dot{D}/\partial D \lessgtr 0$. Have a look at a numerical example with $\mu = 0.3$, $q = 0.3$ and $t = 0.3$. Under these circumstances, if $r < 1$, then $\partial\dot{D}/\partial D < 0$. Empirically speaking, this condition seems to be fulfilled. Henceforth we shall start from the premise $\partial\dot{D}/\partial D < 0$. After that set (17) equal to zero, solve for F and differentiate for D to accomplish:

$$\frac{dF}{dD} \;=\; \frac{(1-t)qr - (1-q)\mu}{(1-q)[\mu + (1-t)r]} \;<\; 0 \tag{18}$$

That is to say, the $\dot{D} = 0$ demarcation line slopes downhill.

At this juncture, we try to find out the $\dot{F} = 0$ demarcation line. The comparison of (1) and (8) yields $\dot{D} + \dot{F} = S$. Get rid of $\dot{D}$ and S with the help of (17) and the savings function:

$$\dot{F} = (1-t)\beta\delta\mu qY - (1-t)qY - (1-t)qrD - \mu qD + [(1-q)(1-t)r - \mu q]F$$
$$- \mu qK + \overline{X} \tag{19}$$

Moreover differentiate (19) for F, which furnishes a critical level of the interest rate as well:

$$r' = \frac{\mu q}{(1 - q)(1 - t)} \tag{20}$$

If $r \lessgtr r'$, then $\partial\dot{F}/\partial F \lessgtr 0$. Beyond that, set (19) equal to zero, solve for F and differentiate for D:

$$\frac{dF}{dD} = \frac{(1 - t)qr + \mu q}{(1 - q)(1 - t)r - \mu q} \tag{21}$$

If $r \lessgtr r'$, then $dF/dD \lessgtr 0$. Put another way, if the foreign interest rate is low, the $\dot{F}$ = 0 line will slope downhill. Conversely, if the foreign interest rate is high, the $\dot{F} = 0$ line will slope uphill.

Let us begin with the case $r > r'$. Composing all building blocks, figure 1 contains the phase diagram. It demonstrates that the crossing of the demarcation lines is a saddle point. Therefore the long–run equilibrium will be unstable. Now regard the situation $r < r'$. The evaluation of (18) and (21) shows that

$$\text{slope } (\dot{D} = 0) > \text{slope } (\dot{F} = 0) \tag{22}$$

Figure 2 presents the pertinent phase diagram. The lesson taught by the directional arrows is that the intersection is a saddle point. Thus, in this case too, the long–run equilibrium will be unstable.

For the remainder of this section, we shall trace out the process of adjustment kicked off by an export shock. Originally the economy is in the steady state. Above all full employment prevails. Both the budget and the current account balance. At the start, let public debt and foreign assets be zero. Then, abruptly, exports deteriorate. In the phase diagram, for the situation $r > r'$, both demarcation lines shift upwards, cf. figure 3. The streamline visualizes how the economy travels through

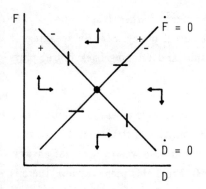

Figure 1
Dynamics of Public Debt and
Foreign Assets ($r > r'$)

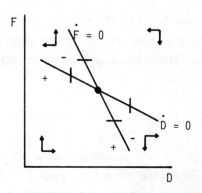

Figure 2
Dynamics of Public Debt and
Foreign Assets ($r < r'$)

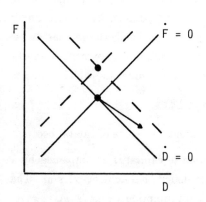

Figure 3
Export Shock and Fiscal Policy

time. In the short term, output falls and unemployment emerges. Instantaneously, to prevent this, the government switches to a loose fiscal policy. Strictly speaking, it elevates public consumption, thereby raising output and bringing back full employment.

In the intermediate term, the budget deficit contributes to the accumulation of public debt. Similarly, the current account deficit contributes to the accumulation of foreign debt. Households refrain from saving, hence private wealth does not answer. That is why private consumption stays put as well. From this point of view, there is no need for fiscal policy to change its stance. Output holds fast, and full employment continues to exist. Eventually, in the long term, public and foreign debt are bound to go off. In the real world, however, the foreign interest rate would climb in response. To conclude, fiscal policy succeeds in always keeping up full employment. On the other hand, public and foreign debt grow without limits, which seems not to be feasible in the long term.

This forms a remarkable contrast to the results obtained for the closed economy, where the long–run equilibrium turned out to be stable (cf. Carlberg 1992, p. 123). To see this more clearly, contemplate a monetary disturbance. At the beginning, the economy is in the long–run equilibrium. The labour market clears, the budget breaks even, and firms abstain from investment. At the start, let public debt be zero. Under these circumstances, the quantity of money diminishes. In the short run, this drives up the interest rate, thus curtailing output and provoking unemployment. Immediately, to absorb this shock, the government augments its purchases, which supports output and restores full employment.

In the medium run, due to the negative investment, the stock of capital becomes dismantled. Owing the $Y = K^{\alpha} \overline{N}^{\beta}$, the contraction of capital is accompanied by a contraction of output. And because of the budget deficit, public debt piles up. The government has to pay more interest, so private consumption expands. As a reaction, the government reduces its purchases. In the end, the economy converges to a new long–run equilibrium. The budget balances again, and firms stop to disinvest. A substantial amount of public debt has been heaped up during transition, whereas private capital has fallen dramatically below its initial level. Phrased differently, there will be heavy crowding out.

6. FISCAL POLICY WITH CONTINUOUS BUDGET BALANCE

To begin with, we shall sum up the findings reached so far. First, under slow money wages, the economy is haunted by the twofold evil of unemployment and long–run instability. Second, continuous budget balance can restore long–run stability. On the other hand, this strategy increases unemployment. Third, monetary policy is able to remedy neither unemployment nor long–run instability, as is well known. Fourth, fiscal policy can defend full employment indeed. However, it cannot overcome long–run instability. Fifth, this suggests the question whether fiscal policy with continuous budget balance is suited to provide both full employment and long–run stability.

Therefore, in the current section, we shall postulate flexible fiscal policy with continuous budget balance. As a response to a shock, the government continuously adjusts public consumption and the tax rate so as to maintain both full employment and budget balance at all times. Accordingly, there is no reason for money wages to change or for public debt to occur. For ease of exposition, we assume that firms do not invest, and that foreign assets are not taxed.

The short–run equilibrium can be characterized by a system of fourteen equations:

$$Y = C + G + X - Q \tag{1}$$

$$Y = K^{\alpha} N^{\beta} \tag{2}$$

$$T = tY \tag{3}$$

$$G = T \tag{4}$$

$$X = (ep^*/p)^{\theta} \tag{5}$$

$$Q = qC \tag{6}$$

$$\dot{F} = X + rF - Q \tag{7}$$

$$Y + rF = C + S + T \tag{8}$$

$$S = \mu(A^* - A) \tag{9}$$

$$A^* = \beta\delta(1-t)Y \tag{10}$$

$$A = F + K \tag{11}$$

$$N = \overline{N} \tag{12}$$

$$w/p = \beta Y/N \tag{13}$$

$$M/p = Y/r^\eta \tag{14}$$

Here α, β, δ, η, θ, μ, e, p*, q, r, w, F, K and $\overline{N}$ are exogenous, while p, t, A, A*, C, F, G, M, N, Q, S, T, X and Y are endogenous. The short–run equilibrium can be viewed as a single differential equation $\dot{F} = f(F)$. In the long–run equilibrium, the accommodation of foreign assets comes to a halt $\dot{F} = 0$.

At this juncture, we shall probe into the stability of the long–run equilibrium. By virtue of $Y = K^\alpha \overline{N}^\beta$, output is invariant since capital and labour supply are constant. Now (1) and (8) imply $\dot{F} = S$. Then substitute (10) and (11) into (9), observing (3) and (4):

$$S = \beta\delta\mu(Y - G) - \mu(F + K) \tag{15}$$

In addition combine this with $\dot{F} = S$ and differentiate for F :

$$d\dot{F}/dF = -\beta\delta\mu dG/dF - \mu \tag{16}$$

Our next job is to eliminate dG/dF. To achieve this, solve (1) for G and note (6), which yields $G = Y - (1 - q)C - X$. Further try to get rid of C and X. Let us start with X. Amalgamate (5) and (13) to conclude $X = (\beta ep^*Y/w\overline{N})^\theta$. The right–hand side is uniform, which can be abbreviated by $X = \overline{X}$. Similarly join (8) and (15), paying attention to (4), and regroup:

$$C = (1 - \beta\delta\mu)(Y - G) + rF + \mu(F + K) \tag{17}$$

After that insert (17) and $X = \overline{X}$ into $G = Y - (1 - q)C - X$ and differentiate for F:

$$\frac{dG}{dF} = - \frac{(1 - q)(r + \mu)}{1 - (1 - q)(1 - \beta\delta\mu)} \tag{18}$$

Finally put this into (16) to arrive at a critical value of the interest rate:

$$r' = \frac{q}{\beta\delta(1 - q)} \tag{19}$$

If $r \lessgtr r'$, then $\dot{F}/dF \lessgtr 0$. That means, when the foreign interest rate is small, the long–run equilibrium will be stable. But when the foreign interest rate is sufficiently large, the long–run equilibrium will be unstable.

Beginning with the stable branch, consider for instance an export shock. Initially the economy is in the steady state. The labour market clears. Both the budget and the current account balance. At the start, let domestic residents hold no foreign assets. In this situation, exports decline. In the short term, this lowers output, so firms have to dismiss workers. Besides the budget moves into deficit. Instantaneously, in order to avoid this, the government raises both public consumption and the tax rate. This in turn advances output, thereby bringing back full employment and budget balance. In the intermediate term, the current account deficit leads to the accumulation of foreign debt. That is why private wealth and private consumption are pulled down. At once, to counteract this, the government pushes up public consumption and the tax rate. Hence output remains unaffected, and full employment as well as budget balance continue to exist. Moreover, the fall in private consumption and imports diminishes the current account deficit. Over time the economy gravitates to a new steady state. Full employment does still prevail. Both the budget and the current account break even. And a certain volume of foreign debt has been heaped up. In a sense, this is the price to be paid for securing full employment.

Now the unstable branch will be sketched out briefly. In the intermediate term, owing to the growth of foreign debt, the interest outflow swells. This enhances the current account deficit, thus accelerating the growth of foreign debt. In the end, foreign debt tends to explode. Clearly this is not feasible in the long term. Beyond that, in the real world, the foreign interest rate would jump up in response.

As a main result, fiscal policy with continuous budget balance always keeps up full employment. Over and above that, it can restore long–run stability.

SYNOPSIS

Tables 5 and 6 present an overview of the conclusions drawn in this monograph, focusing on long–run stability. First have a look at flexible exchange rates in the basic model, cf. table 5. Under flexible, fixed and slow money wages, the long–run equilibrium proves to be stable. The same holds true for monetary policy. When capital gains are allowed for, long–run stability is subject to a condition. If the foreign interest rate is low, the long–run equilibrium will be stable. Conversely, if the foreign interest rate is high, the long–run equilibrium will be unstable. That means, capital gains are a potential factor of long–run instability. In the portfolio model, too, a stability condition applies.

Second consider flexible exchange rates in an economy with public sector, cf. table 6. Under flexible, fixed and slow money wages, the long–run equilibrium turns out to be unstable. In other words, the public sector creates long–run instability. Continuous budget balance restores long–run stability. The other way round, public debt is a factor of long–run instability. For monetary policy, the long–run equilibrium is unstable. Fortunately, monetary policy with continuous budget balance brings back long–run stability. But the two–country model and the portfolio–model suffer from long–run instability.

Third take fixed exchange rates in the basic model, cf. table 5. Under flexible money wages, the long–run equilibrium is stable. Under fixed money wages, on the other hand, a stability condition arises. If the foreign interest rate is small, the long–run equilibrium will be stable. If the foreign interest rate is large, however, the long–run equilibrium will be unstable. That is to say, fixed money wages are a potential factor of long–run instability. Under slow money wages and in the portfolio model, a stability condition prevails as well.

Fourth regard fixed exchange rates in an economy with public sector, cf. table 6. Under flexible, fixed and slow money wages, the long–run equilibrium is unstable. Put differently, the public sector causes long–run instability. Continuous budget balance can reestablish long–run stability. From this point of view, public debt is a factor of long–run instability. For fiscal policy, the long–run equilibrium is unstable. Luckily, fiscal policy with continuous budget balance can reinstall long–run stability.

Fifth we shall do a comparative evaluation of flexible versus fixed exchange rates in the basic model, cf. table 5. Let us begin with flexible money wages. Under both flexible and fixed exchange rates, the long–run equilibrium will be stable. Next assume fixed money wages. Under flexible exchange rates, the long–run equilibrium will be stable again. As opposed to that, under fixed exchange rates, there will be a condition for long–run stability. Put another way, fixed exchange rates are a potential factor of long–run instability.

Sixth we shall confront the two regimes of exchange rates in an economy with public sector, cf. table 6. Let us start with flexible money wages. Under both flexible and fixed exchange rates, the long–run equilibrium will be unstable. What is more, this replicates for fixed money wages. Now imagine continuous budget balance. Under flexible exchange rates, the long–run equilibrium will be stable. Yet under fixed exchange rates, long–run stability will depend on a condition. In this sense, fixed exchange rates are a potential factor of long–run instability.

Table 5

Stability of Long–Run Equilibrium (Basic Model)

	Flexible Exchange Rates	Fixed Exchange Rates
Flexible Money Wages	Stable	Stable
Fixed Money Wages	Stable	Condition
Slow Money Wages	Stable	Condition
Monetary Policy	Stable	
Capital Gains	Condition	
Portfolio Model	Condition	Condition

Table 6

Stability of Long–Run Equilibrium (Economy with Public Sector)

	Flexible Exchange Rates	Fixed Exchange Rates
Flexible Money Wages	Unstable	Unstable
Fixed Money Wages	Unstable	Unstable
Slow Money Wages	Unstable	Unstable
Continuous Budget Balance	Stable	Condition
Monetary Policy	Unstable	
Monetary Policy with Continuous Budget Balance	Stable	
Fiscal Policy		Unstable
Fiscal Policy with Continuous Budget Balance		Condition
Two Countries	Unstable	
Portfolio Model	Unstable	

CONCLUSION

The analysis has been conducted within an IS–LM model of a small open economy, featuring the dynamics of money wages, private capital, public debt and foreign assets. A macroeconomic shock induces an extended process of adjustment that is characterized by unemployment. This in turn requires a dynamic path of monetary and fiscal policy. As a response to the shock, the central bank continuously adapts the quantity of money so as to keep up full employment all the time. And the government continuously accommodates its purchases of goods and services. Can this be sustained? Or will public and foreign debt tend to explode, thereby squeezing private capital down to zero? As a finding, the answer depends on the government budget constraint, the exchange rate regime, the size of the foreign interest rate, the flexibility of money wages and other factors. The present monograph consists of two major parts, flexible exchange rates (part I) and fixed exchange rates (part II). Each part in turn is composed of two chapters, the basic model (chapter I) and the economy with public sector (chapter II).

First of all have a look at the basic model under flexible exchange rates in chapter I of part I. There the investigation has been carried out within an IS–LM model augmented by the dynamics of foreign assets, domestic capital and money wages. In the short–run equilibrium, foreign assets, domestic capital and money wages are given. In the long–run equilibrium, on the other hand, these variables have adjusted completely. Let us begin with the short–run equilibrium. Firms manufacture a homogeneous commodity by making use of capital and labour. Domestic output is determined by consumption, investment, exports and imports. Consider a small open economy with perfect capital mobility. Therefore the domestic interest rate agrees with the foreign interest rate, which is assumed to be constant. Firms maximize profits under perfect competition. As a consequence, the marginal product of capital corresponds to the interest rate. Properly speaking, this yields the desired stock of capital. Similarly, the real wage rate coincides with the marginal product of labour.

Now we come to current account dynamics. Exports are an increasing function of the real exchange rate, while imports vary in proportion to consumption. The current account surplus is defined as the excess of exports and the interest inflow over imports. The current account surplus in turn leads to the accumulation of foreign assets. Next a few words will be said on investment dynamics. Investment serves to close the gap between desired and actual capital round by round. In this sense, investment contributes to the growth of capital. Moreover regard savings dynamics. According to overlapping generations, desired wealth is proportionate to domestic income. By way of contrast, actual wealth is made up of foreign assets and domestic capital. Then savings are used to overcome the discrepancy between desired and actual wealth period by period. Put differently, savings give rise to the formation of wealth. Domestic income and the interest inflow constitute the income of domestic residents, which can either be consumed or saved. Finally contemplate wage dynamics. The rate of change of money wages is a declining function of the rate of unemployment. In addition, the real demand for money is positively correlated with income and negatively correlated with the interest rate. The central bank fixes the nominal quantity of money. In equilibrium, the real supply of money matches the real demand for it.

To sum up, firms employ as many workers as they need to satisfy aggregate demand, given the stock of capital. Firms set prices such that real wages equal the marginal product of labour, given money wages. Prices in turn feed back on aggregate demand via the Keynes effect, so the system is interdependent.

What are the main properties of the long–run equilibrium? The current account balances, so foreign assets do no longer accumulate. Firms abstain from investment, hence the stock of capital ceases to grow. And households do without saving, thus wealth is uniform. All workers have got a job, so money wages stay put. And output holds fast since labour supply is constant. That means, this is the steady state of a stationary economy.

Here a comment is in place. Both in the short–run and in the long–run equilibrium, liquidity preference harmonizes with the interest rate. In the short–run equilibrium, the marginal product of capital deviates from the interest rate. In the long–run equilibrium, however, they agree. Real wages conform with the marginal product of labour, in the short term as well as in the long term. The short–run equilibrium is dominated by aggregate demand, whereas the long–run equilibrium is dominated by aggregate supply.

How is the long–run equilibrium affected by diverse macroeconomic shocks? First, a monetary expansion leaves no impact on capital, output, foreign assets, consumption, exports, imports, the trade account, real wages and the real exchange rate. Only money wages, prices and the nominal exchange rate go up in proportion.

That is to say, the monetary disturbance has no real effects in the long run. Second, a rise in the foreign interest rate lowers capital, output, consumption, exports, imports, net exports, real wages and the real exchange rate. By way of contrast, the disruption raises foreign assets, money wages and prices. Third, an addition to labour supply increases capital, output and consumption proportionately. Conversely, it reduces money wages and prices in proportion. Foreign assets, the trade account, the nominal exchange rate and real wages do not react. Exports, imports and the real exchange rate mount. Fourth, a boost in the preference for future consumption has no influence on capital and output. However, it pushes up foreign assets, consumption and imports. On the other hand, it pulls down exports and the trade account. Money wages, prices and real wages remain untouched, while both the nominal and the real exchange rate fall.

The short—run equilibrium can be compressed to a system of three differential equations in foreign assets, domestic capital and money wages. As a fundamental result, by adopting phase diagram techniques, the long—run equilibrium proves to be stable. To illustrate this, we trace out the process of adjustment generated by a monetary shock. Initially the economy is at rest in the steady state. In particular, all workers have got a job. The current account balances, and firms refrain from investment. At the start, let domestic residents hold no foreign assets. Against this background, the quantity of money diminishes, say because the money multiplier drops. In the short term, domestic currency appreciates. This restrains exports and output, so firms have to lay off workers. The contraction of exports moves the current account into deficit. And the cut in income is accompanied by a cut in investment.

In the intermediate term, owing to the current account deficit, foreign debt piles up. And due to the negative investment, the stock of capital becomes dismantled. By virtue of the unemployment, money wages begin to decline. Competition forces firms to curtail prices, thereby augmenting real balances. The subsequent depreciation stimulates exports and output, hence firms engage more workers. As income recovers, so does investment. After some time, the current account deficit changes into a surplus. As soon as this happens, foreign debt is being paid back. Likewise investment becomes positive, thus replenishing the stock of capital. In spite of that, overemployment will not occur. The underlying reason is that consumption is small and savings are large, which can be attributed to the wealth gap. Eventually the economy converges to a new steady state. Again the labour market clears. Once more the current account breaks even, and firms stop to invest. Strictly speaking, the whole of foreign debt has been retired. And domestic capital comes back to its original level.

So far we dealt with shocks that involved problems like unemployment. Now, in section 4, we address monetary policy, which offers a radical change of perspective. As a response to a shock, the central bank continuously adapts the quantity of money so as to defend full employment. Here the response may be either instantaneous or delayed. As a major conclusion, the long–run equilibrium turns out to be stable. In other words, this strategy is feasible in the long run.

In chapter II, the basic model is extended to include the public sector. The government levies a tax and raises loans in order to finance both its purchases of goods and services and the interest payments on public debt. The budget deficit in turn contributes to the accumulation of public debt. As a principal outcome, the long–run equilibrium is demonstrated to be unstable. This is in clear contradistinction to the basic model, where the long–run equilibrium was stable. That implies, the public sector creates long–run instability.

Take for instance a monetary shock under fixed money wages. Initially the economy is in the steady state. Both the budget and the current account balance. At the start, let all workers have a job, and let domestic residents hold neither government bonds nor foreign bonds. Under these circumstances, the quantity of money contracts. In the short run, domestic currency appreciates. This curbs exports and output, so unemployment emerges. The decline in exports brings the current account into deficit. And the depression of income is associated with a depression of tax earnings, hence the budget moves into deficit. In the medium run, owing to the budget deficit, public debt builds up step by step. And due to the current account deficit, foreign debt piles up. The economy enters a vicious circle, where the government borrows at home in order to finance the interest payments on public debt. As a consequence, domestic residents borrow abroad in order to finance the interest payments on foreign debt. In the long–run, public and foreign debt tend to explode, and unemployment does still prevail.

Now what problems emanate from instability? In the model no problem does exist. Output and wealth are stable, merely public and foreign debt are unstable. This can be ascribed to the fact that the budget deficit is covered by raising loans abroad. In the small open economy, the foreign interest rate does not climb as a reaction. That is why there will be no crowding out of private investment. In the real world, however, as public and foreign debt proliferate without bounds, the economy will not be small any longer. Instead the foreign interest rate goes up, which displaces private investment. Both capital and output deteriorate. As the foreign interest rate grows without limits, capital and output shrink back to zero. Phrased differently, there will be fatal crowding out. Ultimately the economy must break down. Evidently this is not optimal. Sooner or later the government must reduce its purchases of goods and services. The later this happens, the larger the reduction must be.

In section 5, as an exception, we postulate continuous budget balance. As a response to a shock, the government continuously accommodates its purchases so as to always balance the budget. In this situation, the long–run equilibrium will be stable. Compare this to an economy with budget deficits, where the long–run equilibrium was unstable. That means, continuous budget balance restores long–run stability. The other way round, public debt creates long–run instability. Beyond that, in section 6, we assume monetary policy. As a response to a shock, the central bank continuously adjusts the quantity of money so as to maintain full employment at all times. Under these circumstances, the long–run equilibrium will be unstable. Public debt tends to explode, which obviously cannot be sustained. Finally, in section 8, we imagine monetary policy with continuous budget balance. As a response to a shock, the central bank continuously adapts the quantity of money so as to keep up full employment at all times. And the government continuously accommodates its purchases so as to always balance the budget. As a crucial finding, the long–run equilibrium will be stable. Put another way, this approach is feasible in the long–run. Hence monetary policy with continuous budget balance bears the palm.

At this stage, we proceed from flexible exchange rates in part I to fixed exchange rates in part II. Let us begin with the basic model in chapter I. For example, have a look at the dynamics of an export shock under fixed money wages. Initially the economy is in the steady state. The current account balances. At the start, let all workers get a job, and let domestic residents hold no foreign assets. Then, abruptly, exports deteriorate. In the short term, this impairs output, so firms have to dismiss workers. In the intermediate term, owing to the current account deficit, foreign debt accumulates. Wealth, consumption and output descend, thereby aggravating unemployment. Here two opposing forces act on the current account. On the one hand, wealth, consumption and imports decline, thereby lowering the current account deficit. On the other hand, foreign debt and the interest outflow increase, thus raising the current account deficit. What is the net effect? If the foreign interest rate is low, the interest outflow will be small, so the current account deficit shrinks.

In this case, the long–run equilibrium will be stable. Conversely, if the foreign interest rate is high, the interest outflow will be large, hence the current account deficit surges. In this case, the long–run equilibrium will be unstable.

Now suppose that the foreign interest rate is low. Under this condition, the current account deficit depresses wealth and imports, in this way mitigating the current account deficit. The long–run equilibrium will be stable. Over time the economy gravitates to a new steady state. Unemployment persists, whereas the current account breaks even. And a substantial amount of foreign debt has been heaped up during transition. Instead grant that the foreign interest rate is high. Under this condition, the current account deficit elevates foreign debt and the interest outflow, through this channel exacerbating the current account deficit. The long–run equilibrium will be unstable. In due course, foreign debt is impelled to blow up. This in turn drives wealth, consumption, output and labour demand down to zero. Eventually the economy must collapse. In summary, the economy enters a vicious circle of current account deficit, foreign debt and interest outflow. Domestic residents borrow abroad in order to finance the interest payments on foreign debt. This is a remarkable departure from flexible money wages, where the long–run equilibrium was shown to be stable. Phrased differently, fixed money wages are a potential factor of long–run instability.

In chapter II, the public sector is incorporated into the basic model. As a fundamental result, the long–run equilibrium will be unstable. Confront this with the basic model, where a condition for long–run stability was derived. That is to say, the public sector creates long–run instability. To illuminate this, we throw some light on an export shock under fixed money wages. At the beginning, the economy is in the steady state. Let the labour market clear, and let domestic residents hold neither government bonds nor foreign bonds. Then, suddenly, exports diminish. In the short term, this hampers output and occasions unemployment. In the intermediate term, because of the budget deficit, public debt builds up. And by virtue of the current account deficit, foreign debt piles up. In the long term, both public and foreign debt grow without limits.

In section 4, as an exception, we deal with continuous budget balance. As an outcome, long–run stability hinges on a condition. On the one hand, continuous budget balance can restore long–run stability. On the other hand, it increases the fluctuations of income and employment. Put another way, public debt is a factor of long–run instability. Besides, in section 5, we are concerned with fiscal policy. As a response to a shock, the government continuously adjusts its purchases so as to secure full employment at all times. In this situation, the long–run equilibrium proves to be unstable. Over time, public debt proliferates without bounds. Therefore this strategy cannot be sustained. Last but not least, in section 6, we combine fiscal policy and continuous budget balance. As a reaction to a disturbance, the government continuously adapts its purchases and the tax rate so as to maintain both full employment and budget balance at all times. Under these circumstances, long–run stability is subject to a condition. If the foreign interest rate is low, the long–run equilibrium will be stable. If the foreign interest rate is high, however, the long–run equilibrium will be unstable. To conclude, fiscal policy with continuous budget balance always keeps up full employment. What is more, it can bring back long–run stability.

Of course the avenue chosen here is rather simple. Emphasis has been laid on some basic problems, and many aspects are still open to question. For instance, can these theorems be transferred from a stationary to a growing economy? What would occur if public investment were substituted for public consumption? Do the results apply when inflationary expectations are dynamic and not static? Further it might be argued that in the short run technology is characterized by fixed coefficients, thus firms replace marginal cost pricing by markup pricing. How would the time path be modified by this alteration?

RESULT

Let us begin with a regime of flexible exchange rates. First consider an economy without public sector. A macroeconomic shock induces a drawn–out process of adjustment. As a result, the long–run equilibrium will be stable. In the short run, the economy suffers from unemployment. And in the long run, full employment will be regained. Second have a look at an economy with public sector. As a consequence, the long–run equilibrium will be unstable. In the short run, a macroeconomic shock reduces aggregate demand, thereby giving rise to unemployment and a budget deficit. In the long run, the government borrows in order to finance the interest payments on public debt. Ultimately public debt tends to explode, thus squeezing private capital down to zero. In other words, the economy must break down. Third imagine continuous budget balance. As a response to a shock, the government continuously adjusts its purchases so as to always balance the budget. This strategy restores long–run stability, but unemployment emerges during the process of adjustment. Fourth regard monetary policy. As a response to a shock, the central bank continuously adapts the quantity of money so as to maintain full employment at all times. Unfortunately, the long–run equilibrium proves to be unstable. Owing to the budget deficit, public debt accumulates round by round. Obviously this is not feasible in the long–run. Fifth unite monetary policy and continuous budget balance, which safeguards both full employment and long–run stability.

We come now to a regime of fixed exchange rates. First take an economy without public sector. In the short run, a macroeconomic shock involves unemployment and a current account deficit. In the long run, domestic residents borrow abroad in order to finance the interest payments on foreign debt. If the foreign interest rate is low, the long–run equilibrium will be stable. Conversely, if the foreign interest rate is high, the long–run equilibrium will be unstable. Eventually foreign debt proliferates without bounds, so aggregate demand shrinks back to zero. That means, the economy must collapse. Second contemplate an economy with public sector. As a finding, the long–run equilibrium will be unstable. Put differently, public debt grows without limits. Third, continuous budget balance brings back long–run stability. On the other hand, it increases unemployment. Fourth introduce fiscal policy. As a response to a shock, the government continuously accommodates its purchases so as to defend full employment at all times. Unluckily, the long–run equilibrium turns out to be unstable. In the end, there will be fatal crowding out. Fifth join fiscal policy and continuous budget balance. This yields both full employment and long—run stability, granted the foreign interest rate is low.

SYMBOLS

A   private wealth

B   budget deficit, domestic bonds

C   private consumption

D   public debt

E   current account surplus

F   foreign assets, foreign bonds

G   public consumption

H   trade account surplus

I   private investment

K   private capital

L   money demand (real)

M   quantity of money (nominal)

N   labour demand

$\overline{N}$ labour supply

Q   imports

R   real exchange rate

S   private savings

T   income tax

X   exports

Y   output, income

a   wealth–income ratio, savings per head

c   consumption per head

e   exchange rate

f   function

g   function

h   function

j   function

m   money–wealth ratio

p   price of domestic goods

p*   price of foreign goods

q   import rate

r   interest rate

t   tax rate

u   utility

w   wage rate

186

α parameter of production function

β parameter of production function

γ parameter of utility function

δ parameter of utility function

ϵ speed of wage adjustment

η interest elasticity of money demand

θ elasticity of exports

κ speed of money adjustment

λ speed of capital adjustment

μ speed of wealth adjustment

τ time

Π profits

REFERENCES

ABEL, A. B., Consumption and Investment, in: B. M. Friedman, F. H. Hahn, Eds., Handbook of Monetary Economics, Amsterdam 1990

ALLEN, P. R., Financing Budget Deficits, in: European Economic Review 10, 1977, 345 – 373

ALLEN, P. R., A Portfolio Approach to International Capital Flows, in: Journal of International Economics 3, 1973, 135 – 160

ALLEN, P. R., KENEN, P. B., Asset Markets, Exchange Rates and Economic Integration, Cambridge 1980

ALLEN, P. R., KENEN, P. B., Portfolio Adjustment in Open Economies, in: Weltwirtschaftliches Archiv 112, 1976, 33 – 72

AOKI, M., Dynamic Analysis of Open Economies, New York 1981

ARROW, K. J., BOSKIN, M. J., Eds., The Economics of Public Debt, New York 1988

ATKINSON, A. B., STIGLITZ, J. E., Lectures on Public Economics, London 1980

AUERBACH, A. J., KOTLIKOFF, L. J., Dynamic Fiscal Policy, Cambridge 1987

BALTENSPERGER, E., Geldpolitik und Wechselkursdynamik, in: Kredit und Kapital 14, 1981, 320 – 340

BALTENSPERGER, E., BOEHM, P., Stand und Entwicklungstendenzen der Wechselkurstheorie – ein Überblick, in: Außenwirtschaft 37, 1982, 13 – 61

BARRO, R. J., Are Government Bonds Net Wealth?, in: Journal of Political Economy 82, 1974, 1095 – 1117

BAUMOL, W. J., Economic Dynamics, New York 1970

BENASSY, J. P., Non–Walrasian Equilibrium, Money and Macroeconomics, in: B. M. Friedman, F. H. Hahn, Eds., Handbook of Monetary Economics, Amsterdam 1990

BENDER, D. u. a., Hg., Vahlens Kompendium der Wirtschaftstheorie und Wirtschaftspolitik, München 1992

BHANDARI, J. S., PUTNAM, B. H., Eds., Economic Interdependence and Flexible Exchange Rates, Cambridge 1983

BLANCHARD, O. J., FISCHER, S., Lectures on Macroeconomics, Cambridge 1989

BLINDER, A. S., SOLOW, R. M., Does Fiscal Policy Matter?, in: Journal of Public Economics 2, 1973, 319 – 337

BOSKIN, M. J., Ed., Private Saving and Public Debt, Oxford 1987

BOYER, R. S., Devaluation and Portfolio Balance, in: American Economic Review 67, 1977, 54 – 63

BOYER, R. S., Financial Policies in an Open Economy, in: Economica 45, 1978, 39 − 57

BRAINARD, W. C., NORDHAUS, W., WATTS, H. W., Eds., Money, Macroeconomics, and Economic Policy, Cambridge 1991

BRANSON, W. H., The Dual Roles of the Government Budget and the Balance of Payments in the Movement from Short−Run to Long−Run Equilibrium, in: Quarterly Journal of Economics 90, 1976, 345 − 367

BRANSON, W. H., BUITER, W. H., Monetary and Fiscal Policy With Flexible Exchange Rates, in: J. S. Bhandari, B. H. Putnam, Eds., Economic Interdependence and Flexible Exchange Rates, Cambridge 1983

BRANSON, W. H., HENDERSON, D. W., The Specification and Influence of Asset Markets, in: R. W. Jones, P. B. Kenen, Eds., Handbook of International Economics, Amsterdam 1985

BRANSON, W. H., ROTEMBERG, J. J., International Adjustment with Wage Rigidity, in: European Economic Review 13, 1980, 309 − 332

BRUCE, N., PURVIS, D. D., The Specification of Goods and Factor Markets in Open Economy Macroeconomic Models, in: R. W. Jones, P. B. Kenen, Eds., Handbook of International Economics, Amsterdam 1985

BRUNNER, K., MELTZER, A. H., Money Supply, in: B. M. Friedman, F. H. Hahn, Eds., Handbook of Monetary Economics, Amsterdam 1990

BUITER, W. H., Budgetary Policy, International and Intertemporal Trade in the Global Economy, Amsterdam 1989

BUITER, W. H., A Guide to Public Sector Debt and Deficits, in: Economic Policy 1, 1985, 13 − 79

BUITER, W. H., International Macroeconomics, Oxford 1990

BUITER, W. H., Principles of Budgetary and Financial Policy, Cambridge 1990

BUITER, W. H., Short−Run and Long−Run Effects of External Disturbances Under Floating Exchange Rate, in: Economica 45, 1978, 251 − 272

BUITER, W. H., Structural and Stabilization Aspects of Fiscal and Financial Policy in the Dependent Economy, in: Oxford Economic Papers 40, 1988, 220 − 245

BUITER, W. H., Temporary Equilibrium and Long−Run Equilibrium, New York 1979

CARLBERG, M., Fiscal Policy, Berlin 1990

CARLBERG, M., Makroökonomik der offenen Wirtschaft, München 1989

CARLBERG, M., Monetary and Fiscal Dynamics, Heidelberg 1992

CARLBERG, M., Public Debt, Taxation and Government Expenditures in a Grow−ing Economy, Berlin 1988

CARLBERG, M., Theorie der Arbeitslosigkeit, München 1988

CAVES, R. E., FRANKEL, J. A., JONES, R. W., World Trade and Payments, Glenview 1990

CHIANG, A. C., Fundamental Methods of Mathematical Economics, New York 1984

CHIPMAN, J. S., KINDLEBERGER, C. P., Eds., Flexible Exchange Rates and the Balance of Payments, Amsterdam 1980

CHRIST, C. F., On Fiscal and Monetary Policies and the Government Budget Restraint, in: American Economic Review 69, 1979, 526 — 538

CLAASSEN, E. M., Grundlagen der makroökonomischen Theorie, München 1980

COHEN, D., Private Lending to Sovereign States, Cambridge 1991

COHEN, D., DE LEEUW, F., A Note on the Government Budget Restraint, in: Journal of Monetary Economics 6, 1980, 547 — 560

CURRIE, D. A., KATZ, E., A Reconsideration of the Balanced Budget Multiplier, in: Journal of Macroeconomics 1, 1979, 309 — 313

CZERKAWSKI, C. I., Theoretical and Policy—Oriented Aspects of the External Debt Economics, Berlin 1991

DERNBURG, T. F., Gobal Macroeconomics, New York 1989

DERNBURG, T. F., DERNBURG, J. D., Macroeconomic Analysis, Reading 1969

DIAMOND, P. A., National Debt in a Neoclassical Growth Model, in: American Economic Review 55, 1965, 1126 — 1150

DIECKHEUER, G., Internationale Wirtschaftsbeziehungen, München 1991

DORNBUSCH, R., Dollars, Debts, and Deficits, Cambridge 1986

DORNBUSCH, R., Open Economy Macroeconomics, New York 1980

DORNBUSCH, R., Real Exchange Rates and Macroeconomics: A Selective Survey, in: S. Honkapohja, Ed., The State of Macroeconomics, Oxford 1990

DORNBUSCH, R., FISCHER, S., Exchange Rates and the Current Account, American Economic Review 70, 1980, 960 — 971

DORNBUSCH, R., FISCHER, S., Macroeconomics, New York 1993

DORNBUSCH, R., GIOVANNINI, A., Monetary Policy in the Open Economy, in: B. M. Friedman, F. H. Hahn, Eds., Handbook of Monetary Economics, Amsterdam 1990

ETHIER, W. J., Modern International Economics, New York 1988

FELDERER, B., HOMBURG, S., Makroökonomik und neue Makroökonomik, Berlin 1991

FELDSTEIN, M., Ed., The United States in the World Economy, Chicago 1988

FEUERSTEIN, S., Studien zur Wechselkursunion, Heidelberg 1992

FILC, W., Bestandsorientierte Wechselkurstheorien und Wirtschaftspolitik, in: Kredit und Kapital 20, 1987, 48 — 72

FISCHER, S., Recent Developments in Macroeconomics, in: Economic Journal 98, 1988, 294 – 339

FLEMING, J. M., Domestic Financial Policies under Fixed and Floating Exchange Rates, in: IMF Staff Papers 9, 1962, 369 – 380

FLEMMING, J. S., Debt and Taxes in War and Peace: The Case of a Small Open Economy, in: M. J. Boskin, Ed., Private Saving and Public Debt, Oxford 1987

FLOYD, J. E., International Capital Movements and Monetary Equilibrium, American Economic Review 59, 1969, 472 – 492

FRANCKE, H. H., u.a., Möglichkeiten einer binnenwirtschaftlich orientierten Geldpolitik bei weltweit hohen Zinsen, Berlin 1985

FRENKEL, J. A., MUSSA, M. L., Asset Markets, Exchange Rates and the Balance of Payments, in: R. W. Jones, P. B. Kenen, Eds., Handbook of International Economics, Amsterdam 1985

FRENKEL, J. A., RAZIN, A., Fiscal Policies and the World Economy, Cambridge 1987

FRENKEL, J. A., RODRIGUEZ, C. A., Portfolio Equilibrium and the Balance of Payments: A Monetary Approach, in: American Economic Review 65, 1975, 674 – 688

FREY, B. S., Internationale Politische Ökonomie, München 1985

FRIEDMAN, B. M., HAHN, F. H., Eds., Handbook of Monetary Economics, Amsterdam 1990

FRISCH, H., SCHWÖDIAUER, G., Eds., The Economics of Exchange Rates, in: Beihefte zu Kredit und Kapital 6, 1980

FUHRMANN, W., ROHWEDDER, J., Makroökonomik, München 1991

VON FURSTENBERG, G. M., Ed., International Money and Credit, Washington 1983

GAAB, W., Devisenmärkte und Wechselkurse, Berlin 1983

GABISCH, G., LORENZ, H. W., Business Cycle Theory, Berlin 1989

GAHLEN, B., HESSE, H., RAMSER, H. J., Hg., Wachstumstheorie und Wachstumspolitik, Tübingen 1991

GANDENBERGER, O., Theorie der öffentlichen Verschuldung, in: F. Neumark, Hg., Handbuch der Finanzwissenschaft, Tübingen 1981

GANDOLFO, G., Economic Dynamics, Amsterdam 1980

GANDOLFO, G., International Economics, Berlin 1986

GÄRTNER, M., Makroökonomik flexibler Wechselkurse, Berlin 1990

GEHRELS, F., Essays in Macroeconomics of an Open Economy, Berlin 1991

GERLACH, S., PETRI, P. A., Eds., The Economics of the Dollar Cycle, Cambridge 1990

GIAVAZZI, F., SPAVENTA, L., High Public Debt: The Italian Experience, Cambridge 1988

GIOVANNINI, A., The Real Exchange Rate, the Capital Stock and Fiscal Policy, European Economic Review 32, 1988, 1747 − 1767

DE GRAUWE, P., The Economics of Monetary Integration, Oxford 1992

DE GRAUWE, P., Macroeconomic Theory for the Open Economy, Aldershot 1983

GREEN, C. J., LLEWELLYN, D. T., Eds., Surveys in Monetary Economics, Oxford 1991

GRÖßL, I., Der Zusammenhang von finanz− und realwirtschaftlichem Sektor einer offenen, stationären Volkswirtschaft, Berlin 1986

GRÖßL−GSCHWENDTNER, I., Wirkungen staatlicher Budgetdefizite, Tübingen 1990

GRUBEL, H., International Economics, Homewood 1981

GURLEY, J. G., SHAW, E. S., Money in a Theory of Finance, Washington 1966

GYLFASON, T., Fiscal Policy, Long−Run Stability and Aggregate Supply, in: European Economic Review 11, 1978, 99 − 103

HALIASSOS, M., TOBIN, J., The Macroeconomics of Government Finance, in: B. M. Friedman, F. H. Hahn, Eds., Handbook of Monetary Economics, Amsterdam 1990

HAMMANN, D., Zahlungsbilanz, Konjunkturtransmission und Wechselkursbestimmung, Baden−Baden 1980

HANSON, J. A., Growth in Open Economies, Berlin 1971

HARBRECHT, W., Europa auf dem Wege zur Wirtschafts− und Währungsunion, Bern 1981

HEFFERNAN, S., SINCLAIR, P., Modern International Economics, Oxford 1990

HELPMAN, E., RAZIN, A., Dynamics of a Floating Exchange Rate Regime, in: Journal of Political Economy 90, 1982, 728 − 754

HEMMER, H. R., SCHRÖDER, J., Hg., Außerwirtschaft, Göttingen 1988

HENIN, P. Y., Macrodynamics, London 1986

HESSE, H., STREIßLER, E., TICHY, G., Hg., Außenwirtschaft bei Ungewißheit, Tübingen 1985

HEUBES, J., Konjunktur und Wachstum, München 1991

HICKS, J. R., Methods of Dynamic Economics, Oxford 1985

HONKAPOHJA, S., Ed., The State of Macroeconomics, Oxford 1990

HORNE, J., Criteria of External Sustainability, in: European Economic Review 35, 1991, 1559 − 1574

HOWITT, P. The Limits to Stability of a Full−Employment Equilibrium, in: Scandinavian Journal of Economics 80, 1978, 265 − 282

IHORI, T., Debt Burden and Intergeneration Equity, in: K. J. Arrow, M. J. Boskin, Eds., The Economics of Public Debt, New York 1988

ISSING, O., Einführung in die Geldtheorie, München 1991

JARCHOW, H. J., Theorie und Politik des Geldes, Göttingen 1992

JARCHOW, H. J., RÜHMANN, P., Monetäre Außenwirtschaft, Göttingen 1991

JONES, R. W., KENEN, P. B., Eds., Handbook of International Economics, Amsterdam 1985

KATH, D., Geld und Kredit, in: D. Bender u.a., Hg., Vahlens Kompendium, München 1992

KATZ, E., A Note on Bond Finance, Perfect Capital Mobility, and Stability, in: Oxford Economic Papers 29, 1977, 141 – 144

KEMP, M. C., KIMURA, Y., Introduction to Mathematical Economics, New York 1978

KENEN, P. B., The International Economy, Englewood Cliffs 1985

KEYNES, J. M., The General Theory of Employment, Interest and Money, London 1936

KLAUSINGER, H., Zur dynamischen Makro–Theorie einer offenen Wirtschaft, in: J. H. Pichler, Hg., Strategien der Wechselkurspolitik, Berlin 1986

KLEIN, M., Zentralbankinterventionen an effizienten Devisenmärkten, Hamburg 1985

KÖHLER, C., POHL, R., Hg., Währungspolitische Probleme im integrierten Europa, Berlin 1992

KONRAD, A., Zahlungsbilanztheorie und Zahlungsbilanzpolitik, München 1979

KRAUSE–JUNK, G., Ed., Public Finance and Steady Economic Growth, The Hague 1990

KRELLE, W., Theorie des wirtschaftlichen Wachstums, Berlin 1988

KRUEGER, A. O., Exchange Rate Determination, Cambridge 1983

KRUGMAN, P. R., Exchange Rate Instability, Cambridge 1988

KRUGMAN, P. R., OBSTFELD, M., International Economics, New York 1991

KÜLP, B., Außenwirtschaftspolitik, Tübingen 1978

KUSKA, E. A., On the Almost Total Inadequacy of Keynesian Balance–of–Payments Theory, in: American Economic Review 68, 1978, 659 – 670

LACHMANN, W., Fiskalpolitik, Berlin 1987

LEHMENT, H., Fiskalpolitik in offenen Volkswirtschaften, Tübingen 1988

LORENZ, H. W., Nonlinear Dynamical Economics and Chaotic Motion, Berlin 1989

LUCAS, R. E., Models of Business Cycles, Oxford 1987

LUCKENBACH, H., Internationale Wirtschaftspolitik, München 1993

MACDONALD, R., TAYLOR, M. P., Exchange Rate Economics, in: C. J. Green,

D. T. Llewellyn, Eds., Surveys in Monetary Economics, Oxford 1991

MALINVAUD, E., Profitability and Unemployment, Cambridge 1986

MANKIW, N. G., Macroeconomics, New York 1991

MARSTON, R. C., Stabilization Policies in Open Economies, in: R. W. Jones, P. B. Kenen, Eds., Handbook of International Economics, Amsterdam 1985

MASSON, P. R., Dynamic Stability of Portfolio Balance Models of the Exchange Rate, in: Journal of International Economics 11, 1981, 467 − 477

McCALEB, T. S., SELLON, G. H., On the Consistent Specification of Asset Markets in Macroeconomic Models, in: Journal of Monetary Economics 6, 1980, 401 − 417

McCALLUM, B. T., Monetary Economics, New York 1989

McCANDLESS, G. T., WALLACE, N., Introduction to Dynamic Macroeconomic Theory, Harvard 1992

McKINNON, R. I., Portfolio Balance and International Payments Adjustment, in: R. A. Mundell, A. K. Swoboda, Eds., Monetary Problems of the International Economy, Chicago 1969

McKINNON, R. I., OATES, W. E., The Implications of International Economic Integration for Monetary, Fiscal and Exchange−Rate Policy, in: Princeton Studies in International Finance 16, 1966

MEADE, J. E., The Balance of Payments, London 1951

MEIJDAM, L., VAN STRATUM, R., Dynamic Adjustment and Debt Accumulation in a Small Open Economy, in: Journal of Economics 51, 1990, 1 − 26

MODIGLIANI, F., The Debate Over Stabilization Policy, Cambridge 1986

MOHR, E., Economic Theory and Sovereign International Debt, New York 1991

MUNDELL, R. A., International Economics, New York 1968

MURATA, Y., Mathematics for Stability and Optimization of Economic Systems, New York 1977

MUSSA, M., A Model of Exchange Rate Dynamics, in: Journal of Political Economy 90, 1982, 74 − 104

NEUMANN, M., Theoretische Volkswirtschaftslehre, München 1991

NEUMANN, M. J. M., Ed., Monetary Policy and Uncertainty, Baden−Baden 1986

NGUYEN, D., TURNOVSKY, S. J., The Dynamic Effects of Fiscal and Monetary Policies under Bond Financing, in: Journal of Monetary Economics 11, 1983, 45 − 71

NIEHANS, J., International Monetary Economics, Oxford 1984

OATES, W. E., Budget Balance and Equilibrium Income, in: Journal of Finance 21, 1966, 489 − 498

OBSTFELD, M., Macroeconomic Policy, Exchange Rate Dynamics, and Optimal

Asset Accumulation, in: Journal of Political Economy 89, 1981, 1142 – 1161

OBSTFELD, M., STOCKMAN, A. C., Exchange–Rate Dynamics, in: R. W. Jones, P. B. Kenen, Eds., Handbook of International Economics, Amsterdam 1985

OHR, R., Budgetpolitik in offenen Volkwirtschaften, Berlin 1987

OTRUBA, H., MUNDUCH, G., STIASSNY, G., Makroökonomik, Wien 1992

PAPADEMOS, L., MODIGLIANI, F., The Supply of Money and the Control of Nominal Income, in: B. M. Friedman, F. H. Hahn, Handbook of Monetary Economics, Amsterdam 1990

PAPADOPOULOU, D. M., Makroökonomik der Wechselkursunion, Frankfurt 1993

PERSSON, T., Global Effects of National Stabilization Policies under Fixed and Floating Exchange Rates, in: Scandinavian Journal of Economics 84, 1982, 165 – 192

PERSSON, T., SVENSSON, L., Current Account Dynamics and the Terms of Trade, in: Journal of Political Economy 93, 1985, 43 – 65

PESEK, B. P., SAVING, T. R., Money, Wealth and Economic Theory, New York 1967

PHELPS, E. S., Effectiveness of Macropolicies in Small Open–Economy Dynamic Aggregative Models, in: W. C. Brainard et al, Eds., Money, Macroeconomics and Economic Policy, Cambridge 1991

PICHLER, J. H., Hg., Strategien der Wechselkurspolitik, Berlin 1986

POHL, R., Theorie der Inflation, München 1981

PORTES, R., SWOBODA, A., Eds., Threats to International Financial Stability, Cambridge 1987

PRACHOWNY, M. F. J., Macroeconomic Analysis for Small Open Economies, Oxford 1984

REITHER, F., Nachfrageschocks und Wechselkursvolatilität, in: Kredit und Kapital 25, 1992, 55 – 64

RODRIGUEZ, C. A., Short– and Long–Run Effects of Monetary and Fiscal Policies Under Flexible Exchange Rates and Perfect Capital Mobility, in: American Economic Review 69, 1979, 176 – 182

ROSE, K., SAUERNHEIMER, K., Theorie der Außenwirtschaft, München 1992

ROSE, M., Finanzwissenschaftliche Makrotheorie, München 1980

RÜBEL, G., Factors Determining External Debt, Berlin 1988

SACHS, J. D., The Current Account in the Macroeconomic Adjustment Process, in: Scandinavian Journal of Economics 84, 1982, 147 – 159

SALOP, J., SPITÄLLER, E., Why Does the Current Account Matter?, in: IMF Staff Papers 27, 1980, 101 – 134

SAMUELSON, P. A., NORDHAUS, W. D., Economics, New York 1992

SARGENT, T. J., Dynamic Macroeconomic Theory, Cambridge 1987

SARGENT, T. J., Macroeconomic Theory, Boston 1987

SAUERNHEIMER, K., Internationale Kapitalbewegungen, flexible Wechselkurse und gesamtwirtschaftliches Gleichgewicht, Hamburg 1980

SCARTH, W. M., Bond—Financed Fiscal Policy and the Problem of Instrument Instability, in: Journal of Macroeconomics 1, 1979, 107 – 117

SCARTH, W. M., Fiscal Policy and the Government Budget Constraint under Alternative Exchange—Rate Systems, in: Oxford Economic Papers 27, 1975, 10 – 20

SCARTH, W. M., Friedman's Framework for Economic Stability and the Government Budget Constraint, in: Manchester School 50, 1982, 231 – 247

SCHÄFER, W., Währungen und Wechselkurse, Würzburg 1981

SCHÄFER—LOCHTE, C., Makroökonomik der J—Kurve, Frankfurt 1993

SCHMID, M., Fiscal Ponzi Games in a World Economy, in: F. Gehrels et al., Eds., Real Adjustment Processes under Floating Exchange Rates, Berlin 1990

SCHMID, M., Fiscal Strategies, Foreign Indebtedness, and Overlapping Generations, in: E. Streißler, Ed., Structural Problems and International Trade

SCHMIDBERGER, W. D., Fiskalpolitik in kleinen offenen Volkswirtschaften, Hamburg 1983

SCHMITT—RINK, G., BENDER, D., Makroökonomie geschlossener und offener Volkswirtschaften, Berlin 1992

SCHRÖDER, J., Haushaltsdefizit und Wechselkurs in einem Güter—Finanzmarkt—Modell, in: H. R. Hemmer, J. Schröder, Hg., Außenwirtschaft, Göttingen 1988

SIEBERT, H., Außenwirtschaft, Stuttgart 1984

SIEBERT, H., Foreign Debt and Capital Accumulation, in: Weltwirtschaftliches Archiv 124, 1988, 618 – 630

SIEBKE, J., THIEME, H. J., Einkommen, Beschäftigung, Preisniveau, in: D. Bender u.a., Hg., Vahlens Kompendium, München 1992

SINN, H. W., International Capital Movements, Flexible Exchange Rates, and the IS—LM Model, in: Weltwirtschaftliches Archiv 119, 1983, 36 – 63

SITZ, A., Schockübertragung und Wechselkurssystem, in: J. H. Pichler, Hg., Strategien der Wechselkurspolitik, Berlin 1986

SMEETS, H. D., Der monetäre Ansatz der Zahlungsbilanztheorie, Frankfurt 1982

SMITH, G., Flexible Policies and IS—LM Dynamics, in: Journal of Macroeconomics 4, 1982, 155 – 178

SOHMEN, E., Wechselkurs und Währungsordnung, Tübingen 1973

STEIN, J. L., International Financial Markets, Cambridge 1991

STEIN, J. L., Monetarism, Amsterdam 1976

STEIN, J. L., Monetarist, Keynesian and New Classical Economics, New York 1982

STIGLITZ, J. E., On the Relevance or Irrelevance of Public Financial Policy, in: K. J. Arrow, M. J. Boskin, Eds., The Economics of Public Debt, New York 1988

STOCKMAN, A., SVENSSON, L., Capital Flows, Investment, and Exchange Rates, in: Journal of Monetary Economics 19, 1987, 171 – 201

THIEME, H. J., Geldtheorie, Baden–Baden 1987

TIVIG, T., Flexible Wechselkurse aus der Sicht des Finanzmarktansatzes, Berlin 1991

TOBIN, J., Asset Accumulation and Economic Activity, Oxford 1980

TOBIN, J., The Monetary–Fiscal Mix: Long–Run Implications, in: American Economic Association, Papers and Proceedings 76, 1986, 213 – 218

TOBIN, J., BUITER, W. H., Long–Run Effects of Fiscal and Monetary Policy on Aggregate Demand, in: J. L. Stein, Ed., Monetarism, Amsterdam 1976

TOBIN, J., de MACEDO, J. B., The Short–Run Macroeconomics of Floating Exchange Rates: An Exposition, in: J. Chipman, C. Kindleberger, Eds., Flexible Exchange Rates and the Balance of Payments, New York 1981

TURNOVSKY, S. J., Macroeconomic Analysis and Stabilization Policies, Cambridge 1977

TURNOVSKY, S. J., The Asset–Market Approach to Exchange Rate Determination: Some Short–Run, Stability, and Steady–State Properties, in: Journal of Macroeconomics 3, 1981, 1 – 32

TURNOVSKY, S. J., The Dynamics of an Open Economy with Endogenous Monetary and Fiscal Policies, in: Weltwirtschaftliches Archiv 115, 1979, 201 – 223

TURNOVSKY, S. J., The Dynamics of Fiscal Policy in an Open Economy, in: Journal of International Economics 6, 1976, 115 – 142

TURNOVSKY, S. J., On the Formulation of Continuous Time Macroeconomic Models with Asset Accumulation, in: International Economic Review 18, 1977, 1 – 27

TURNOVSKY, S. J., International Macroeconomic Stabilization Policy, Oxford 1990

TURNOVSKY, S. J., Intertemporal Issues in International Macroeconomics, in: Journal of Economic Dynamics and Control 15, 1991, 1 – 3

TURNOVSKY, S. J., Ed., Intertemporal Issues in International Macroeconomics, Amsterdam 1991

TURNOVSKY, S. J., Macroeconomic Analysis and Stabilization Policies, Cambridge 1977

WAGNER, H., Stabilitätspolitik, München 1989

WELLISCH, D., Intertemporale und internationale Aspekte staatlicher Budgetdefizite, Tübingen 1991

WENZEL, H. D., Defizitfinanzierung als Instrument einer zielorientierten Finanzpolitik, Baden–Baden 1983

WESTPHAL, U., Makroökonomik, Berlin 1988

WILLMS, M., Internationale Währungspolitik, München 1992

WOHLTMANN, H.W., Quantitative Wirtschaftspolitik bei alternativen Erwartungen, Frankfurt 1987

ZEE, H. H., The Sustainability and Optimality of Government Debt, IMF Staff Papers 35, 1988, 658 – 685

ZIESCHANG, M., Finanzmarktansätze der Wechselkurserklärung, Berlin 1990

INDEX

Printing: Weihert-Druck GmbH, Darmstadt
Binding: Buchbinderei Schäffer, Grünstadt